NECHAKO COUNTRY

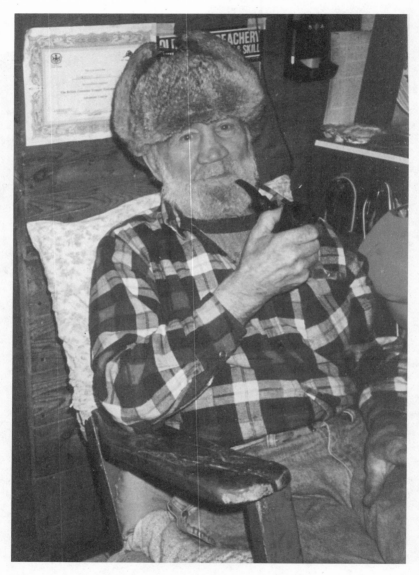

Bert relaxes in his favourite old rocking chair, 2003.

NECHAKO COUNTRY

IN THE FOOTSTEPS OF BERT IRVINE

JUNE WOOD

VANCOUVER • VICTORIA • CALGARY

Heritage House Publishing Company Ltd.
#108–17665 66A Avenue   PO Box 468
Surrey, BC V3S 2A7   Custer, WA
www.heritagehouse.ca   98240-0468

Library and Archives Canada Cataloguing in Publication

Wood, June, 1945–
    Nechako country: in the footsteps of Bert Irvine/June Wood.

ISBN 978-1-894974-27-1

    1. Irvine, Bert. 2. Vanderhoof Region (B.C.)—History. 3. Nechako River Valley (B.C.)—History. 4. Vanderhoof Region (B.C.)—Biography. 5. Nechako River Valley (B.C.)—Biography. I. Title.

FC3845.N43Z49 2007   971.1'8204092   C2006-906976-X

Library of Congress Control Number: 2006940147

Edited by Carolyn Boyd and Jonathan Dore
Proofread by Marial Shea
Cover design by Jacqui Thomas
Interior design and layout by Darlene Nickull
Cover and all interior photos courtesy of the author

Printed in Canada

Heritage House acknowledges the financial support for its publishing program from the Government of Canada through the Book Publishing Industry Development Program (BPIDP), Canada Council for the Arts, and the province of British Columbia through the British Columbia Arts Council and the Book Publishing Tax Credit.

The Canada Council | Le Conseil des Arts
for the Arts | du Canada

BRITISH
COLUMBIA
ARTS COUNCIL
We acknowledge the support of the Province of British Columbia
through the British Columbia Arts Council

This book has been produced on 100% post-consumer recycled paper, processed chlorine free and printed with vegetable-based dyes.

To my dad, Bert Irvine

CONTENTS

FOREWORD

Growing up, as I did, on the beautiful, pristine banks of the Nechako River was an experience that has given me a deep respect for the power and sanctity, and also the fragility, of our Mother Earth. When I was young I lived in a world where everyone and everything in Mother Nature seemed so interconnected and so precious.

My world was peopled with unique characters, living in community and harmony in ways that I rarely see today. The people I remember were full of energy, ideas, enthusiasm, conversation and respect for all life. Many were ranchers and other country folk who were adopted as "aunts" and "uncles" by us, as my daddy brought this very southern custom with him to Canada. Figuring largely in this unique family of mine were the Irvines and the Reeds. Whenever I see their faces, in all of those snapshots and vignettes of memory, I feel rich and full.

What I remember most is the joy of debate, argument and conversation that everyone shared. I can still see my mother, Gloria, and "Uncle" Bert (Irvine) locked in debate at the old kitchen ranch table, fists pounding for emphasis, the arguments expanding and circling, while watching adults (and us children) laughed and laughed. Uncle Bert is one of the most formidable and stubborn debaters I have known, with the possible exception of my mother. I count it a great privilege to have grown up listening to them argue about everything from the character flaws/strengths of some politician to the appropriate height of a bedroom window.

Uncle Bert is an ingenious and well-trained carpenter, with very strict ideas about what is "done" and what is simply "not done," and up until my mother's death in 1986, he did all her carpentry work, renovating and building new rooms and patios, adding skylights, a Jacuzzi and so on. My mother, however, was an interior decorator who had unconventional ideas, so building projects were always another source of debate. What fun we all had listening to them! I remember clearly one discussion in the late 1970s, when I was home on a visit from Vancouver. Uncle Bert was renovating a room in our house, and they argued for two days over the colour of the filing cabinet. Gloria eventually won; to this day it remains a ruby red.

My mom, Uncle Bert, "Aunt" Mary Irvine and Daddy (known as "Uncle Rich" to many, including my mother) were all known as "kindliness personified" to children in an era when corporal punishment and severe discipline were the norm. They were champions of young people and were the ones many would turn to in times of distress. With this in mind I look back to the humour kindly Uncle Bert used to control some of us "handfuls." He has a pair of twin nephews, Stan (Junior) and David Irvine, and a niece, Patty, with whom I grew up. The boys especially were lively little ones, with a never-ending supply of mischief up their sleeves. Bert, who never hit a child in his life, with laughter in his eyes and humour in his voice, would threaten us all with his "board with the rusty nail" (which purportedly carried some previous malefactor's dried blood) if we didn't stay in line. We never felt any fear or really believed him—but we minded, just the same.

What a gift June has given us all. Her work as a naturalist, fighting to save the Nechako River (and the myriad forms of life that rely upon it) from extinction is well known. Her chronicle of her family, of those whose lives they have touched and of their combined love and respect for Mother Nature is an inspiration.

Thank you, June, for your dedication, for your tenacity and for this wonderful book.

Cathy Hobson

Cathy is the daugher of esteemed author Rich Hobson, who wrote Grass Beyond the Mountains, Nothing Too Good for a Cowboy *and* The Rancher Takes a Wife.

ACKNOWLEDGEMENTS

The road from rough manuscript to published book is long and bumpy—at least it was for me. For years, this book was a tiny, restless seed in my mind, waiting to germinate and grow. I wasn't sure how to begin. For one thing, I couldn't decide if I should tell my dad's story using his voice or if I should write in the third person. Then I had a chance meeting with the late Cynthia Wilson, who owned Caitlin Press in Prince George, and I told her about the indecision that was preventing me from getting started. She said, "Don't worry about that. Just start writing." I did. Later, Cynthia's words of encouragement gave me the confidence to continue writing.

As I stumbled along the bumpy road, an angel appeared in the form of Susan Reese. Discouraged, I had set aside my manuscript for many months. One warm summer day I went to the computer and brought up my book. Minutes later, as I was having a problem with the computer, a knock came at the door—a rare occurrence when one lives 60 kilometres from town. There stood Susan Reese and her husband, Dave. Susan asked if she could use our satellite phone to call a tow truck, explaining that they had driven quite a distance with two flat tires, which they believed were beyond repair. As it turned out, not only was Susan something of a computer expert, but she was also a poet and had done some editing. She was very interested in this book I was writing. I printed off a copy of my manuscript and she took it home to Oregon with her. Words of praise and constructive criticism followed, giving me the motivation I so sorely needed at that point in time. Thank you, Susan, for your unfaltering support over the past few years.

I am indebted to Chris Czajkowski for the insight she gave me into the world of publishing and for reading my rough manuscript and saying, "I definitely think you have a good book here." These positive words coming from the talented, accomplished writer that Chris is made me believe that my writing was good enough for publication. Thank you, Chris.

Thanks to Diana Wilson, former editorial assistant at the Heritage Group, who gave me the wonderful news that Heritage House publisher Rodger Touchie had given the go-ahead on my manuscript. Diana, who is originally from Vanderhoof and the niece of a character ("Smitty") mentioned in Nechako Country, gave me valuable guidance, helping me to pare the manuscript down to bring my dad into clearer focus. She was always very supportive, and I appreciate the role she played in Heritage's accepting my book for publication.

Once on the editing road, I worked with substantive editor Carolyn Boyd, which resulted in a major reorganization of the manuscript and, I hope, an improved book. Thanks, Carolyn! Then, when I thought I was finished, Jonathan Dore copyedited the manuscript, going over it with a fine-toothed comb and making me dig still deeper. Thank you, Jonathan! And, finally, thanks to managing editor Vivian Sinclair, for your sensitivity while we worked through the final edits and for your good-natured diplomacy throughout this long project.

A special thank you to Cathy Hobson for writing the foreword for Nechako Country; I appreciate the time you took from your busy life, Cathy, to write the warm and generous words that you did.

Many thanks to Neal Erhorn, Don Hogarth and Barb Mazereuw (formerly Weinhardt) for sharing their recollections of family and a bygone time; to Walter Wigmore and Paul Angelo for writing out (in longhand) their colourful stories; to Larry Erickson for his poignant reflections (and photo contributions); to Uncle Stan for relating some of the more humorous times he remembered from "the heyday of guiding"; to Linda Sjodin (my sister) for reading my early manuscript and offering bits of information I'd forgotten; a big thank you to my mom, Mary Irvine, for writing out some of her lighter moments as chief cook and bottle-washer of the outfit!

I would be very remiss if I didn't acknowledge the unfailing support of my husband, Denis, who did not begrudge the time I spent writing—and the time he spent as my "sounding board"—over the past several years. Thank you, Denis.

Of course, this book would not exist if it weren't for my dad. Although he kept a journal during his early days on the trapline, somewhere along the way that journal was lost. As a result, I was left to rely on his amazing memory, going back to the early 1930s. This meant countless interviews to dredge up details and get stories straight. Regardless, I expect that he will point out some small discrepancy when he reads the finished product. Thanks for your patience, Dad. I hope you like the book.

PREFACE

The Chipewyans called him Wabanukasus. In their language this meant "he who travels by night." The slight young trapper earned this name because he had the habit of travelling all night, especially when a full moon lit the way. He walked, snowshoed, mushed his dog team or rode horseback to reach his destination—be it Whitecourt, Iosegun Lake or one of his far-flung trapline camps. Mekamonia, translating as "red-faced white man," was a name the Cree pinned on the young trapper. No doubt the moniker was apt; being of fair skin he was often sunburned from long days spent out in the elements, even though he always wore a brimmed hat. Mixing with the Cree and Chipewyan enabled him to learn enough of their languages to be able to communicate and get along well with them, learning their ways. Wabanukasus to the Chipewyan or Mekamonia to the Cree was Bert Irvine, my dad.

The impetus for me to write this book was a long-smouldering desire to tell my dad's story—a story of a way of life that has all but vanished. His was, and still is, a life intertwined with the wilderness, one of independence and doing things "his way." After moving his young family—my mom, my sister Linda and me—from Barrhead in northwestern Alberta to Vanderhoof in central British Columbia, the upper Nechako country and the Nechako River became an integral part of our lives. Because it is so ingrained in us, the country itself is a major player in this story, as are the people who have come and gone through the years, particularly the Hobsons, and of course the tortured Nechako River that is the lifeblood of our beloved Nechako country.

NECHAKO COUNTRY

While this story spans the years from 1934 to 2005—a period of unprecedented and fast-paced change—much of it is focused on the 1950s and '60s. The wilderness way of life that I recount in these pages has been replaced by a new world of high technology, and the wilderness itself has been pushed back and badly bruised. This story gives a glimpse into simpler times and into the life of an indomitable spirit, Bert Irvine.

CHAPTER 1

ALBERTA BEGINNINGS

DISCOVERING IOSEGUN

The vast, rolling, muskeg-laced country that lies between Barrhead and Sturgeon Lake in northwestern Alberta is an area encompassing some 12,000 square miles. My dad, Bert Irvine, planned to be in that sizeable chunk of wilderness the summer of 1934. He was 15 years old and the plan was to rendezvous with his uncle, Wes Reed, at Lone Pine, a small settlement northwest of Barrhead. Wes was the fire ranger cum game warden for that immense, unsettled area and had agreed to let my dad accompany him to help clear the network of trails that were necessary to keep an eye on the country, watching for forest fires and illegal hunting.

Wes was a swarthy, well-built little man with a real air of confidence about him—a take-charge kind of guy. His big, dark eyes, like those of most of the Reed family, looked out from under bushy eyebrows, and a generous slash of a mouth creased his leathery face. He'd been a sniper in World War One, twice wounded, and had cut a handsome figure in his uniform. The older Wes got, the bushier his eyebrows grew, and with a slightly balding head he wasn't quite as handsome as he'd been in earlier years. But he never lost his air of complete confidence, and this showed in the way he carried himself. He was not a man with

1

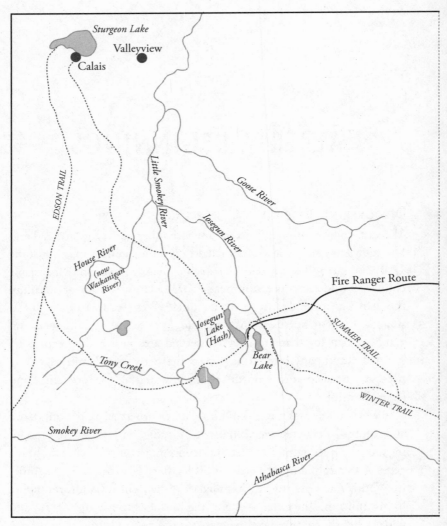

Hash Lake and Area, Alberta:

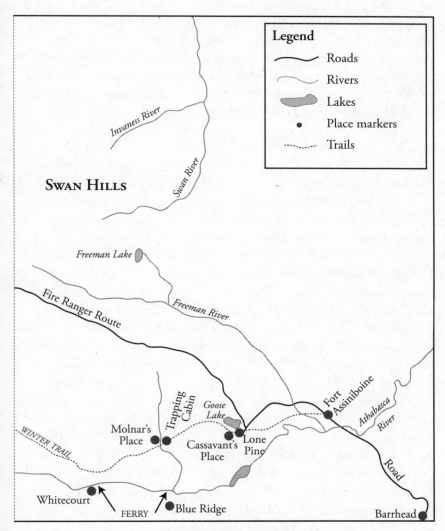

Trails and Roads in the 1930s

great patience for inept or lazy people. Quite likely, Wes's experience as a sniper had influenced his personality and accounted, in part, for his gruff demeanour. His sister Bertha Irvine, my dad's mother, called Wes "the mogue." There is no such word as mogue in the dictionary, but in her usual imaginative way, my grandmother may have conjured up this title as a spin on the word "mogul"—an important, powerful or influential person. In other words, Wes was the head honcho of the outfit. Wes would become an exemplary role model—a mentor for the wilderness way of living, trapping and surviving off the land that would encompass my dad's entire life.

Dad bore no resemblance to Wes and the Reed side of the family. He was of average height, about 5 feet 11 inches, of very slender build with fair skin, sandy-brown hair and twinkling blue eyes that spoke of his enthusiasm for life and his boundless energy. He'd inherited his colouring from his father, David Irvine, a fair-skinned Scotsman who'd come over from the Orkney Islands when he was in his late twenties. Dad's nose had been badly broken just several months before leaving home to travel with Wes. While pleasure-riding with his schoolteacher, his horse had thrown its head; my dad's nose wouldn't be reconstructed till years later, so it is hard to say whose features he'd inherited.

School finally let out and my dad threw his pack and well-worn snowshoes into his parents' 1929 Pontiac, bound for Lone Pine. Wending their way north, my dad and his parents took the ferry across the Athabasca at Holmes Crossing, about a mile downstream from Fort Assiniboine, and then drove westward, finally arriving at the Cassavants'. The Cassavant family operated a blacksmith shop at their homestead about a mile from the post office, the end of the road. The post office, operated by the Carty family, was Lone Pine in its entirety. Mr. Cassavant was formerly the blacksmith in Barrhead, and the family warmly greeted their weary friends. But there was no sign of Wes. Dave and Bertha headed for home early the next morning, leaving their son to settle in with the Cassavants while he waited for Wes to show up. This was not much of a hardship—he and the Cassavant boy were looking forward to fishing some of the area lakes. As it turned out, this was a good thing, because it wasn't until a full month later that Wes rode into the yard on his horse Babe, with his pack horse Smokey in tow. Wes had had something that was of far higher priority on his mind than meeting his nephew on schedule at Lone Pine—he'd been courting Dorothy Madsen in Whitecourt!

Now it was finally time to hit the trails that intersected those thousands of square miles of rolling boreal forest. These trails skirted fish-filled lakes fed by beaver-dam-riddled streams and mosquito- and blackfly-infested muskeg. Dad and Wes took turns riding Babe and walking while leading Smokey. Some of the trails they followed were old Native trails worn deep by centuries of use; others Wes had cut himself. And then there were new trails to be blazed and cut. When windfall blocked the way, which it frequently did, they used a Swede saw to cut through the fallen trees. Camp for the night was always made by water: a lake, creek or river that would provide fresh fish for supper and would have grass along its perimeter for the horses. Building a smudge fire was the first task at hand upon stopping for the night—this helped to keep the flies from driving the horses crazy as they filled their bellies on the lush grass and pea vine.

The job of fire ranger and game warden specified that 15 miles per day must be covered; progress was to be recorded in a logbook and handed in at the ranger station in Whitecourt every two weeks. My dad and Wes frequently travelled up to 40 miles a day before stopping at some prime fishing spot to rest up for a day or so. But when they arrived in Whitecourt on schedule every two weeks to hand in the logbook, the entries *clearly* indicated that they'd covered a steady 15 miles each day.

Whitecourt was a thriving frontier town boasting two sawmills, Western Construction and Whitecourt Sawmill, which employed many of the town's 500 or so inhabitants. There were two general stores, each owned by one of the mills, and Western Construction also owned the ferry that Wes—and, later, also my dad—operated when they were in town. They stayed in a cabin Wes owned, situated high on a cutbank overlooking the powerful Athabasca. When someone wanted to cross the river on the ferry, as my dad put it, "We had to run like hell down the hill!" Whitecourt also had a post office, a hotel, a big livery stable, a forestry office and a rooming house that "had girls."

The summer trail from Hash Lake to Whitecourt ran through where the oil town of Fox Creek stands today, but there was no settlement there then. The country was a pristine wilderness where moose, deer, grizzlies, black bear and fur-bearing animals were plentiful, roaming the country with little disruption from human endeavours. Waterfowl in flocks of thousands blackened the skies, their collective and varied cries creating a natural symphony for all living things to enjoy.

The months spent on the trail with Wes, enjoying time together around the campfire, hearing the comforting tinkle of the horses' bells as they grazed contentedly in the distance and lying at night listening to the sound of the breeze whispering through the trees, whet Dad's appetite for more; he wanted more of this wonderful new country so rich in wildlife, more of its challenges. The wilderness and all it held had seeped into his very being, and he had no desire to return to the close confines of the classroom in Barrhead. He'd made up his mind; he'd be on the trapline with Wes next winter. Wes had spent the previous two winters trapping along Christmas Creek, about 80 miles northwest of Barrhead; in those winters, he'd either camped out on the trail or stayed in his dugout. But because Dad was planning on coming back with him, he decided to rent a cabin that belonged to a fellow who had done some homesteading but now lived in Fort Assiniboine. This would be much better for both of them, because they'd have a permanent base camp from which to operate.

Not surprisingly, my grandparents were not happy with their son's decision to quit school and go trapping. Not that he lacked experience; he'd been trapping since he was nine years old, when he and his family had moved from Old Barrhead to New Barrhead. The railway had just been built through the country, but it didn't pass through Old

Barrhead, which at the time boasted a blacksmith, a big log rooming house, a garage and Thurston's general store. The Irvines were the first family to move their house from Old Barrhead to the new townsite. The house sat right on the Klondike Trail, and, like many, they had used a team of horses to skid their house the three miles to the new location. New Barrhead was not only on the railway, but it was also located along the meandering Paddle River. My dad was drawn to the river, and spent most of his free time there, skating and skiing its winding course, trapping muskrats. Muskrat pelts were worth about 60 cents apiece at the time—a welcome supplement to a farm income—so many of the homesteaders trapped them. My dad's Uncle Fred, one of Wes's brothers, had a cabin on his quarter section of land at Sandy Lake, where Dad and his younger brother, Bill, stayed for days at a time. Sometimes Allan and Norman, Wes's other two brothers, would also be there trapping. My dad didn't start going to school till he was almost nine years old—when he and his family moved to New Barrhead. In other words, he learned to trap before he learned to read and write.

As a boy, my dad learned to be very independent, through trapping and also because of his time away from his parents. During the summer his father went to other communities, such as Westlock and Mayerthorpe, or even up to the Peace River country, to build grain elevators. My dad's mother often went along on these building excursions, taking young Marguerite with her. Dad and Bill would stay behind for the summer, under the wing of their grandmother, Kate Reed. Dad wasn't tied to his mother's apron strings by any stretch of the imagination, so the idea of being away for the winter didn't bother him in the least.

As preparations for the move to the trapline heated up in fall 1934, Grandma Kate decided it would be a good idea if she spent the winter with her son and oldest grandson at Christmas Creek. She would do the cooking and keep the fires going when the boys were on the trail tending to their traps and shooting squirrels or hunting. No one was about to argue with her decision, but it meant they wouldn't be walking to the cabin. Snow had come early, so Norman volunteered to use his sleigh and team of horses to take them in. Not only would my dad, Wes and Kate be along for the ride, but also Dorothy Madsen, who had ridden her buckskin out from her home in the Christmas Creek area and would be accompanying them back, sometimes riding her horse and sometimes riding in the sleigh. Kate, who was close to 70 at the time, was settled into the sleigh under a deep covering of buffalo robes to keep her warm for the 80-mile trip. My dad, Wes and Dorothy alternated riding the lively buckskin, but when they arrived at the small settlement of Christmas Creek, close to where the creek flows into the Athabasca, my dad struck off across country, riding Dorothy's horse to the Madsen place. Wes, Dorothy and Norman continued on the road with the sleigh and made it all the way to Madsen's—a distance of about 60 miles from Barrhead—by that night. This was considered something of a record. They were greeted by Wes's three sleigh dogs, strays he'd picked up around Barrhead and left at Madsen's that fall. The next day the remaining 20 miles were covered by sleigh to the cabin at Christmas Creek. The cabin was a good size, with a veranda across the front, and it looked very welcoming as they pulled into the small grassy opening where it sat. Supplies were unloaded, fires lit in the heater and cookstove, and it wasn't long before Kate had a meal started. Home for the winter was looking pretty good.

Wes's trapline stretched about 15 miles up the creek, to where he had a dugout cabin in the creek bank. Because grassy openings lined the sides of the creek, the main bank where he had excavated his dugout was quite a long way back from the water's edge. A dugout is similar in structure to a root cellar. Wes's dugout was quite large and had a stove and bunks, making a very primitive, but welcome, shelter after a cold day on the trail. He planned on using the dugout again that winter, so there would be times when he wouldn't be back to the cabin for several days.

Survival in the wilderness depends on innovation and using every talent you possess—and there was nothing Wes couldn't do when he put his mind to it. He had built a sled the winter before, steaming pieces of oak to make the wood supple enough for runners that curved up at the tips, and during the long nights spent alone he'd fashioned dog harnesses by braiding strips of rawhide. He left the sled and harness at the dugout when he went out in early spring. Now, with the dogs he'd brought in, he had the beginnings of a team, so he could put the sled and harness to work. The dogs weren't huskies, but they'd do for now.

Although my dad sometimes accompanied Wes checking his traps, he had his own line a little closer to the cabin, about 8 miles up and down the creek. At that time there was no such thing as a registered trapline; all you needed was a trapping licence and you were free to set traps wherever you wanted, as long as you weren't infringing on someone else's territory. Dad snowshoed his line daily that winter, trapping mink, weasel (ermine), coyotes and a few fox; he also shot a lot of squirrels with his .22. Life was great, especially with Grandma Kate doing the cooking and the aroma of freshly baked bread greeting him when he arrived home at night, tired after a long day on the trail. They ate well. Moose were plentiful in the area, and Wes had shot one for their winter meat supply. Rabbit and beaver meat provided an occasional welcome change.

Most long evenings were spent carving more stretching boards, and skinning, stretching and turning fur. When enough pelts had been accumulated to make a trip worthwhile, Dad and Wes went out to Blue Ridge to sell their catch. Blue Ridge, about 20 miles to the south on the other side of the Athabasca, had a sawmill and a couple of stores, one of which bought furs. Dad spent the proceeds of his catch on a new gun, a Savage bolt action that boasted a clip and a peep site. Winter was pleasantly wearing on, but Kate was beginning to wonder how she was going to get home. Late in the winter it was decided to take her by dogsled to the home of friends, the Molnars, who lived only a few miles away on Christmas Creek. Kate stayed with the Molnars for several weeks before Wes took her, again by dogsled, to the Cassavants' home, where Dave and Bertha picked her up in the Pontiac. My dad and Wes stayed on to trap a few spring beaver before calling it a season. The winter had been a success.

Back home in Barrhead, my dad spent the spring doing carpentry work with his father, but when summer rolled around it was time to hit the trails with Wes again, to carry out the duties of fire ranger and game warden. They covered a tremendous amount of country in their travels, making camp alongside favourite lakes or creeks and rivers filled with fish, as they followed the trails that were their responsibility to keep open. Although they revelled in all the untamed virgin countryside they travelled through, they were particularly impressed with a lake the Cree called Iosegun.

Iosegun is a Cree word meaning "all hashed up"; thus the slang name for the lake, Hash, came to be used interchangeably with Iosegun. The lake lay within the unspoiled country bounded by the mighty Athabasca to the south, the Little Smoky River to the east and the Iosegun River to the west. About four miles long, the lake had all the qualities that would make it a good place to locate permanently: there was a healthy beaver population, fish were plentiful, and fringing its west end were slough-grass meadows where horses could rustle in winter. While the Cree did some trapping in the area, their main settlement was at Sturgeon Lake, some 80 miles to the northeast. A very old Cree told my dad that he could remember when moose first moved into the Iosegun Lake area about 50 years earlier; they were now abundant, as were mule deer. Hunting would be good. The lake was on the path of an international flyway, so in spring and fall the sky and the lake were alive with waterfowl, and the trilling of huge flocks of sandhill cranes circling overhead added to nature's symphony in this virtual Eden that was soon to become their home.

They would share this paradise with the animals that lived here, the animals they would trap and hunt. Trapping was their livelihood. They hunted when they needed meat, but they had great respect for nature and lived in harmony with it, never taking too much and never wasting.

Hash Lake Days

Wes and Dad's long summer on the trails, carrying out the game warden and fire ranger duties, had cemented their idea of putting down roots at Hash Lake. The fall of 1935 saw them in Barrhead preparing for the pack trip to take in supplies for building a cabin; nails, roofing material, sheet metal with which to make a stove, and even glass for the windows would all be packed onto the horses. Wes was also preparing for another event—his marriage to Dorothy Madsen, whom he'd been courting for the past year. Dorothy was a woman of many talents, who would make an ideal life partner for Wes. She was a good horsewoman, an artist, she played the guitar and the mouth organ, and, on top of all that, she was a great cook. But perhaps most importantly, she loved the wilderness and the trapper's way of life. She was as eager as Wes and my dad to get to the lake and begin the task of carving out a new home.

Summer still lingered in the air that wonderful September, making the trip to the lake a pleasant one. Dad, Wes and Dorothy had scouted the lake's perimeter that summer, searching for the best location to build their cabin. There were several candidates, but in the end they chose a location with lovely clumps of birch scattered across an otherwise open area. It faced south across the lake—a winning attribute because the southern exposure would be good for growing a garden. Natural meadows lay just beyond the building site, and beyond the meadows was a good stand of spruce timber. Another selling point was that the spot was on a fairly high bank, so it wouldn't be subject to flooding, as some of the lower-lying areas would in high-water years. These things together convinced them they'd chosen the perfect spot for their new home.

The dense stand of spruce from which the trees for the cabin were cut lay about a quarter-mile from the building site, beyond the natural meadow and willow flat. Felling the 60 trees required to build the 14-by-20-foot cabin was done by hand, using a Swede saw, making this a big part of the building project. Using both horses and dogs to skid the logs, they found that a team of 10 to 12 dogs could pull more than a horse. Once the logs had been moved, the next task was to whipsaw them into lumber for the floor, roof, ceiling and miscellaneous items such as window frames, door frames and a door. When that labour-intensive job was done, the rest of the logs were whipsawed in half for the walls, the flat sides being used on the inside. To help with the job, Wes constructed a trestle-like structure on which the logs were placed; the "push guy" stood on top of the frame, while the "pull guy" was on the bottom. Dad was on the pull end, getting all the sawdust down his neck, while Wes was on the push end, up on the trestle. After hours of this gruelling work, much to Wes's annoyance, my dad would sometimes pause to watch the geese and other waterfowl frolicking on the choppy waters of the lake that stretched out before them. Wes was a hard taskmaster, and he had no patience for frivolity that took away from finishing the job at hand. Birdwatching definitely fell into the frivolous category. Spending so much time with Wes at an impressionable age no doubt helped to mould Dad's character and influence his outlook on life.

With the good weather holding and enthusiasm running high, it wasn't long before a lovely little cabin, complete with a screened-in porch, stood looking out over the lake. Wes had fashioned a heater from the sheet metal they had packed in from Barrhead, but one item of great importance was missing—a cookstove. This meant that a trip to Whitecourt was in order. The weather had turned cold and by early November the muskegs were frozen and covered in snow, allowing Wes to take his dog team over the winter trail to Whitecourt. If the snow wasn't too deep it would be possible to make 9 miles an hour with the dogs, but it still meant Wes would be making camp somewhere along the trail that night. The winter trail was about 10 miles shorter than the summer trail, which had to circumnavigate the network of muskegs and swamps that lay between Iosegun Lake and Whitecourt. In my dad's words, the summer trail "was crookeder'n hell!" The dogs were happy to be in harness, and so it was amid great yipping and yapping that Wes and his dog team glided out of the yard, bound for Whitecourt.

While Wes was away, Dad spent the time getting in a wood supply, which entailed using a Swede saw to cut down the standing dead trees and saw them into stove lengths. The blocks of wood were then loaded into a deep-sided toboggan and pulled by dog team back to the cabin. While Dad was busy cutting wood, Dorothy began to add her womanly touch to the interior of the cabin. Larry Erickson, a young fellow who trapped with Wes and Dorothy years later, described Dorothy's decorating abilities: "The old cabin was a work of art with an almost fairy-tale appearance. The inside was papered. Most furniture was handmade. The cupboards were made from old wooden boxes painted with flowers, horses and things and had homemade wooden hinges and clasps."

Wes was a sight for sore eyes when he pulled back into the yard, the sleigh loaded down with the new cookstove. With its installation the cabin was complete, and the happy trio settled into their new life at Iosegun Lake. This was now their country to do as they pleased, to explore and to trap. The Cree occasionally passed through the area trapping, but their main settlement was at Sturgeon Lake. The only other inhabitants in the area were the Whites, a couple who had a place at Bear Lake (now named Raspberry Lake), about six miles away. They had been there for a few years, and had a good garden established and a barn for their team of horses. Years later, when the war broke out and "the authorities" came in to talk to Mr. White, he objected to the requirement that his gun be registered and to giving out information about himself. He left the area and was later seen in Whitecourt. His wife wasn't with him, however, and this set off an investigation by the RCMP, who rode in and searched their place, finding all of Mrs. White's clothing and other belongings still in the house. It looked very suspicious, but the RCMP was never able to turn up any positive clues as to Mrs. White's strange disappearance.

Dogs played a leading role in life at the lake, their houses scattered along the perimeter of the yard. Any visitor arriving at the place was greeted with a chorus of howling, yapping dogs, straining and leaping at the ends of their chains. Dogs on the loose would chase game, and this could not be tolerated. Such is life with a dog team. Wes kept anywhere from 10 to 12 dogs and Dad kept 5 or 6, sometimes using only 2 to pull his sleigh. Other times he'd simply put packs on them and travel that way. He bought his first sled dog, Rex, from a fellow in Whitecourt who raised the dogs for Admiral Byrd's famous Antarctic expeditions. Rex was a reject. One day, when my dad was in Whitecourt, he saw Rex single-handedly pulling a sled loaded with five or six kids. He gave the kids five dollars, with which they were happy, and Rex was his. Rex more than pulled his weight in the next few years. He was a great dog, but when the Second World War broke out and Dad enlisted in the army, he had no choice but to leave him with his dad and mom in Barrhead. Rex got to killing chickens and chasing livestock on the farms bordering town, so unfortunately that was the end of the great Rex.

One spring day it occurred to Wes and Dad that wolves would make good sleigh dogs, and to that end they stole two wolf pups from the den while their mother was away hunting. All went well till the pups were about a year old; then one of them took a leap at Wes's throat and hit the end of his chain just short of making contact. Wes decided right there and then that domesticating the pups wasn't going to work out, and he shot them both. This was a sad day for everyone, but especially so for Dorothy, who had become very attached to the wolves. They had been allowed to run free around the yard some of the time, but being chained for even short periods must have built up a smouldering resentment in the young animals; with freedom and the wild life inherent in them, the confinement and indignity of being chained was obviously too much for them. But before Wes disposed of them they had mated with some of his female dogs, which produced litters of wolf-cross puppies, and these turned into excellent sleigh dogs.

It takes a lot of food to keep a pack of hungry dogs fed, and as a result, one of the regular chores was setting and checking fish nets in the lake. The nets were 1,000 feet long and 4 to 5 feet wide, with a mesh size of about 4½ inches. In the winter it was important to get the net to sink to the bottom, because if the floaters touched the ice they'd freeze to it, making it difficult to get the net out. Sometimes the net froze in and couldn't be retrieved until the ice went out in spring. Using a jigger or running line, you'd let down the net through a hole chopped in the ice and then put an ear to the ice to figure out where the net had ended up. At that location, you'd cut another hole and pull the string attached to the floaters up through the hole.

Hash Lake supported populations of jackfish, pickerel, tulabee, whitefish, ling cod, suckers and perch. The dogs ate whatever variety of fish they were offered, but mostly they were fed whitefish. The whitefish were far out in the deepest parts of the lake, but they came close to shore in November to spawn in the shallower water. This made them easier to catch. Nets were also set at known "sucker holes" with good results. The dogs were fed once a day, amid great howling, yapping and leaping as each dog was tossed one fish, weighing about seven pounds. When the dogs were in the harness working, they were fed less—and never until reaching the evening camp; a dog with a full stomach feels lazy and won't work as hard.

Keeping the human larder stocked also took time and energy, but one day my dad lucked out. Wes and Dorothy had gone to Whitecourt, leaving Dad alone at the cabin. Enjoying the luxury of privacy, he decided it would be a good time to take a bath. Climbing out of the little tub, he glanced out the kitchen window, and there was a moose browsing the edge of the yard. Stark naked, Dad grabbed his rifle, opened the flap on the large ventilation hole behind the stove and shot the unsuspecting animal. Quickly getting dressed, he ran out, gutted the moose and, since it was −30° F, decided that he'd just roll it over on its back, and that would be good enough for the time being.

Wes and Dorothy, now accompanied by my dad's brother Bill, pulled into the yard by dogsled the next day—and there was the moose, frozen stiff, with its legs sticking straight up in the air. Photographer that she was, Dorothy was not going to let this photo-op pass her by. The moose's decidedly balky stance gave Dorothy an idea—to put a halter on the frozen animal and get Dad to look as if he was coaxing him to lead while Bill applied encouragement from behind. And so the photo "Halter Breaking the Moose" came to be. Dorothy developed her own film, which meant they got to see photos soon after they were taken rather than having to make a trip to town to drop the film off and another to pick up the pictures. As the main photographer of the group, Dorothy took an amazing number of pictures, recording the interesting life that she, Wes and my dad led during their wonderful years together at Hash Lake.

A herd of nine or so horses was quickly built up at the lake. Wes started with Babe and Smokey, then two mares, Silver and Nelly, were added, as well as a stud Wes bought from a Cree. Before long there were foals in the spring, one of them being Prince, a strong dark bay colt that Wes gave to my dad. For the first few years the horses were wintered at Alan and Bessie Reed's farm northeast of Barrhead. In early winter Dad would move the horses, single-handedly, from Hash Lake to Barrhead, a distance of about 120 miles. He changed riding horses often to keep them from tiring and in doing so made good time (as usual—to my dad, everything's a race and a challenge). In the spring he would return to Barrhead and bring the horses—oat-hay fed and raring to go—back to Hash Lake for the summer. This pattern was followed for a few years until Wes and Dad started putting up hay on the wild meadows that skirted parts of the lake. Initially this was done by hand with a scythe, the hay being left in big coils that could later be dug out of the snow and hauled down the frozen lake by dog team. Wes built a sleigh especially for this purpose. The back-breaking work of making hay with a scythe was later eliminated when a horse-drawn mower was packed in from Sturgeon Lake—quite an undertaking, because the mower had to be completely disassembled before packing it onto the horses for the arduous trip in to the lake.

Grandma Kate loved it at Hash Lake, and coming for visits in the dead of winter was a challenge she relished. Wes brought her in by dog team from Sturgeon Lake during some cold weather—it was 40 below when they pulled into the lake, but Kate was in high spirits. She also spent many summers there until she was well into her eighties. Her visits were always welcome. She was an easy guest, a great cook and she helped wherever she could.

The Cree from Sturgeon Lake started coming into Hash Lake to trap and, being a sociable bunch, invited my dad and Wes and Dorothy to come to the "Indian Sports Days" at Sturgeon Lake—the big social event of the summer. Deciding to make the trip with a small string of horses, they camped among the Natives and a few other white settlers on the meadows at Sturgeon Lake. The settlement of Sturgeon Lake was a Hudson Bay post, so supplies could be bought and furs sold there, making the trip to the sports day even more worthwhile. In addition to the HBC post there was another store and fur buyer, making it a popular destination for trappers and homesteaders. Although Sturgeon Lake and Whitecourt were about the same distance from Hash Lake, 70 to 80 miles, the Athabasca River didn't have to be crossed to get to Sturgeon Lake, and there was a post office at the small settlement of Calais, located on the lake. Hash Lake was in the middle, with Whitecourt, located on the south bank of the Athabasca, to the southwest, and Sturgeon Lake to the northeast.

The various competitions at the Indian Sports Days were great fun. Wes was a pretty good wrestler, so he took part in that competition and did well. Other events were the Native women's tug-of-war, tug-of-war on horseback, musical chairs on horseback and weight-pulling matches with teams of horses. Horses were an integral part of everyday life and played a major role in the sports days' activities.

The moccasin telegraph must have been working well, because not long after the Cree began coming to Hash Lake to trap, a group of Chipewyan people rode into the area from Rocky Mountain House, brandishing what they called a letter from the Queen, a long scroll (perhaps a treaty document from the reign of Queen Victoria) proclaiming their right to go anywhere they pleased. The men had long braided hair intertwined with coloured wool, were clothed in buckskins and rode horses—a sign of prosperity. The Cree often walked in summer, sometimes with packs on their dogs, and travelled by dog sled in winter. A few years later some Metis from Lac St. Anne also started to do some trapping in the Hash Lake area, so the country was being fairly heavily trapped, and the trails were well travelled.

The Chipewyans taught Dad the fine art of making snowshoes, one of life's necessities on the trapline. Just the right piece of green birch had to be searched out, then split, whittled, bent to shape and left to dry behind the stove. When the pieces were dry, they were secured together at the toe and tip, and cross pieces were put in place just the right distance apart. These pieces, to which the harness was bound, helped the snowshoe hold its shape and gave it added strength. Finally, the rawhide webbing, the "babiche," which they made themselves from hides, was woven on and laced into the holes made for this purpose along the length of the frame. Lighter-weight rawhide made from deerskin was used to mesh the toe and tail section, while the heavier moose rawhide strips were used in the middle section, the area that bears the user's weight and takes the most punishment. The end result was a beautiful pair of snowshoes that served the trapper well for many years, needing only occasional repairs to the webbing—a favourite meal for squirrels and pack rats.

A trapper must use all his wiles and knowledge if he is to be successful at his trade. Castor, a substance from a beaver's scent gland, is often used both to attract animals and to camouflage human scent. My dad and Wes mixed castor with rotten fish on their mink sets; highly scented anise seed was mixed with rodium oil, and oil of catnip was used to attract lynx. Fur-bearing animals are attracted to large spruce trees because of the shelter they provide, so often they are chosen as a set location. A "covey"—a small shelter, usually of spruce boughs—is built around the trap at the base of the tree. Bait is placed at the back of the covey, and the trap in front. A good trapper checks his traps regularly, every few days. Sometimes the trap has been "sprung" and needs resetting, sometimes the animal is still alive and must be put out of its misery. Most often, the animal is dead and frozen when the trap is checked, but if left too long another animal will come along and eat or damage the animal in the trap, making the hide worthless.

Muskrat were plentiful in Hash Lake, and my dad saved the tails of his bountiful catch to give to the Native kids, who cooked them up and then chewed on the fatty treat with great relish. The Cree and Chipewyan children looked forward to visits from my dad, the Cree calling him Mekamonia, meaning "red-faced white man," and the Chipewyan, Wabanukasus, which roughly translates as "he who travels by night."

Wes, and in turn my dad, adopted many of the Aboriginal ways, preferring the Native style of making camp, which meant erecting wicki-ups rather than tents, even in the dead of winter. A wicki-up is a lean-to-style pole frame over which a covering is laid. Wicki-up is a Cree term, *wicki* meaning "quick"—in other words, it is quick to put up when on the trail. With the open side facing a campfire that stretches the length of the shelter, there is none of the dampness of a tent, and the frame can be left in place at frequently used camping spots. At the end of a long day on the trail, making camp simply requires laying a tarp or spruce boughs over the waiting frame.

The Cree and Chipewyan also constructed tipis. These were of two types: those that were at permanent camps had tanned hides stretched across the poles, while those erected at seasonal trapping and rest spots along the trail were covered in logs, bark and moss. They both had the typical opening at the top where the poles gathered to allow the smoke from the campfire to escape. All materials to build these shelters were from the land—from nature—and sleeping and living in them bonded the inhabitant to the earth.

Wildlife encounters are an inevitable part of life in the bush, and my dad had his share. Once, he was travelling with horses up the Little Smoky River and when he came out into a small opening the horses spooked. He soon saw the reason why: a big grizzly was charging toward him across the clearing. Having been on a beaver-shooting expedition, he was carrying only his .22, but he managed to get three shots off from horseback. The grizzly immediately turned, churning through the big diamond willows like a bulldozer, branches and bushes flying in all directions before disappearing. Dad was sure at least one of his shots had made contact, but when he and Wes returned to the spot the next day to check things out, they could find no sign of blood or the bear.

Another time, my dad was checking his line up the Little Smoky and needed meat, so he was hoping to shoot a moose. Hearing the sound of splashing as an animal walked toward him down the river, he quickly climbed a big tree that hung out over the water, giving him a good vantage point. Instead of a moose, three grizzlies came wandering up the river. As Dad sees it now, "I was just a kid, and like a fool, took a shot at one of them!" Again he was carrying only a .22. Fortunately, the three grizzlies hightailed it back down the river and Dad continued on his way.

The grizzlies that inhabited that part of the country were the huge Plains subspecies of grizzly that had once inhabited the prairies. They'd been pushed into the Swan Hills and Hash Lake areas by encroaching settlement and the clearing of land for agriculture. These areas have now been inundated with seismic lines, oil wells and people; the grizzlies are no longer doing well.

Life in the bush is never dull, and such it was at Hash Lake. Aside from tending traps, skinning and stretching fur, caring for the dogs and horses, making hay, growing a garden and picking wild berries—the daily tasks required for survival in the bush—summer meant forest fires. Wes and my dad were in the thick of things. There was a manned lookout on House Mountain, to the northwest, and when smoke was spotted the information was radioed down to Wes on his crystal radio set at Hash Lake. He and Dad would then strike out on foot or on horseback to check out the area where smoke had been seen and decide if it was serious enough to warrant getting a crew in—no small undertaking. This is where Wes and my dad's hard work keeping the trails open paid off. If the fire looked like it was going to turn into something serious, they'd head directly for Whitecourt, some 80 miles away by the summer trail, to round up a crew—usually patrons of the bar at the hotel—and arrange for a string of pack horses. Phil Myers, a plump little bachelor who owned the livery stable in Whitecourt, was often hired as the packer. Phil kept a string of about 15 horses and 5 or 6 mules to hire out, mainly for fires. He was a good horseman, and always travelled with his pack string.

Putting out the wildfires required a lot of back-breaking shovel work, but Wes and Dad weren't usually on the end of the shovels. Dad's job was to get the pack string and crew into the fire location and then supervise the camp and the crew. Wes was the fire ranger, so he was kept busy with strategizing and radio communications. Of course, there were times when it was necessary for everyone to be on the end of a shovel. There were never any fires in the immediate vicinity of Hash Lake during those years, so being away from the lake for up to a month at a time was the normal situation in summer. All ground fires had to be put out before the area was left, and this sometimes extended over the whole summer and into the fall.

Cabin fever was setting in pretty good after about three years of living in close quarters, so my dad decided it was time to put a little distance between himself and Wes and Dorothy. There was a spot he liked at the other end of the lake, near the outlet of Fox Creek, and this is where he decided to build a cabin of his own. Constructed from unpeeled spruce logs about 10 to 12 inches in diameter, the cabin measured 12 by 12 feet and had one window, across which was stretched a piece of deer hide, oiled to allow some light to filter through. Ten-inch logs, squared on three sides, produced a smooth, solid floor. Split logs formed the inside layer of the roof, over which were placed layers of spruce bark, and then soil. While this wasn't a true sod roof—the type that prairie settlers made—it was a variation of that type. A door was fashioned from an old toboggan. The pole bunk that stretched across one end of the cabin was cushioned by a layer of spruce boughs covered with loose hay. The spruce boughs were frequently replaced to keep the "mattress" springy and fresh. Wes was good at working with metal, and he made my dad a stove by bending a piece of sheet metal and riveting it into an oblong shape that was four feet long and two feet wide. Given the dimensions of the cabin and the size of the stove, the place must have felt like a sauna! Pies, bannock and whatever else needed baking were cooked in the stove by letting the fire burn down to a few embers and then placing the item to be baked inside the stove on top of the embers. Utilizing the old toboggan and constructing the stove were typical of the inventiveness that's necessary when living far from civilization; you simply use what's at hand. There's satisfaction in doing that. The cabin was a true wilderness dwelling, fabricated, for the most part, from what nature had to offer.

A very old Cree kept a dugout canoe at Iosegun Lake to use for spring beaver and muskrat trapping. He let Dad use the canoe, and when the old man finally decided he was getting too old to trap, he gave it to my dad. The 15-foot dugout, carved from a big cottonwood, was pretty tippy, but glided easily through the water. Sometimes Dad put a sail on it, making good time this way on his frequent trips over to Wes and Dorothy's place at the other end of the lake. Most afternoons the lake was whipped into a sea of frothing whitecaps, but the dugout was unsinkable; even if it filled with water, it floated along just beneath the surface, so it could still be paddled. Depending on the weather, this was either refreshing or highly uncomfortable, but over the course of the summer, my dad and that dugout became as one.

About 1939, it became a requirement for every trapper to have a registered trapline. My dad took out a line on the Little Smoky River, in open, rolling country about 10 miles southwest of Hash Lake. Some Cree had built a fairly big cabin on the river and told Dad he was welcome to use it. Early one spring after the snow had gone, he had just pulled into the cabin when he started feeling very sick. Things went from bad to worse, and for a whole week he lay on the bunk in the cold cabin, soaked in sweat and delirious with fever. He ate nothing and was too weak to get up, even to light a fire in the stove. When the fever finally broke and he was preparing to leave for the trip back to Hash

Lake, in pulled Wes with horses. My dad was five days overdue and Wes had come to look for him. Travelling alone, far from civilization, is a risky proposition, and it is a standard rule of the bush that upon departure, a date for your return is given to someone. There is always a little flexibility acknowledged to allow for unforeseen circumstances cropping up, as they so often do. One day late is considered almost on time; five days is leaving it a little long, and Wes could easily have been met with a very different scenario when he reached that cabin on the Little Smoky River.

Interesting events often interjected themselves into normal life on the trapline. Wes was travelling with his dog team on the Edson trail one cold winter day when he heard a plane go down. It didn't take him long to find the downed plane and its pilot in a little meadow at the junction of the Tony and Little Smoky rivers. The pilot wasn't hurt, but his plane needed repairs. Wes took him by dogsled to Hash Lake so that he could use the crystal radio set to call Edmonton for parts. The necessary parts were flown in several days later, and Wes mushed the pilot back to the crash site and helped him make the repairs. Then off the pilot flew again. Apparently, he had just laid around the whole time he was at the lake and had an air about him suggesting that Wes and Dorothy should be honoured by his presence. His not offering to help with any of the chores didn't sit well with Wes, who was of the opinion that there is no room for lazy or arrogant people in the bush.

WINDS OF CHANGE

Over the course of the years from 1934 to 1942, my dad became a well-honed bushman. But come summer he'd head for Barrhead to do carpentry work with his father, who'd brought the tools of his trade with him when he came over by ship from the Orkney Islands. While Dad now considered Hash Lake and the bush his home, working with his father was an opportunity to make a little extra money, and it was a valuable apprenticeship in carpentry. He and his dad helped build the first hospital in Barrhead, and worked on schools, grain elevators and other construction jobs around town. This all ended when the Second World War broke out. Dad walked the 150 miles from Hash Lake to Grande Prairie to enlist, but once there he was told to wait for his "call." Since he'd walked so far, he decided to take a room in a hotel for a few days and hobnobb with the local blacksmith and some of the old-timers around town. Then he walked the 150 miles back to Hash Lake.

When the call to enlist finally came, Dad went to Dr. Vereau for his physical examination. Knowing my dad's medical history, Dr. Vereau offered to write a letter of pardon for him. At 15, my dad had broken his nose while horseback riding, resulting in an infection and the loss of the nose bridge. At the time, Dr. Vereau, the family doctor, had come to the family home in Barrhead, where my dad lay wracked with pain from the infection. He had a ferocious headache. Dr. Vereau said there was no point in admitting him to the hospital since the infection was by this time draining from his nose in copious amounts and surgery was out of the question. It would be five years before Dr. Hepburn at the University Hospital in Edmonton fashioned a new bridge from one of my dad's ribs. At about the same time as the nose-breaking event, Dad was chopping down a tree in the schoolyard and cut his foot with the axe, severing some tendons; his right foot never grew after that, and from then on he referred to it as his "crippled" foot. Although handed the opportunity to stay behind, my dad, true to form, said, "No thanks, I want to join up."

Dad took his basic training at Camrose, Alberta, then field artillery training at Brandon, Manitoba. (After three months training in the army he decided that he didn't like the way they operated, so he quit and enlisted in the RCAF instead.) He wanted to become a fighter pilot, but lack of education kept him from achieving that goal. Dad had only a grade-eight education, and it was those with the highest education who were chosen to become pilots. The skills he'd learned in the bush didn't count for much with the RCAF. I'm sure my dad would have made a superlative pilot had he been given the chance, since he had the right qualities—courage and the ability to think quickly. Instead he was posted to Rivers, Manitoba, then Brandon—where there was a big Air Force base—then Portage La Prairie, Moncton, and Dartmouth, where he worked in the canteen. He was at Halifax when the war ended and he got his discharge. He enjoyed the work and the camaraderie of the canteen, and he and his friends frequently went to the big dances in Winnipeg when he was stationed at Rivers and Brandon. It was here that he met Mary, a pretty Ukrainian girl who worked in Winnipeg as a doctor's receptionist. Fate had played its hand, and my dad and mom were married in Winnipeg on April 26, 1942.

Dad was anxious to introduce his new bride to Wes and Dorothy, so on his first leave they headed for Sturgeon Lake, where Wes and Dorothy were camped, taking in the Indian Sports Days. Dad and Mom travelled as far as High Prairie by train and then caught the mail truck, driven by one of the Reimer family, whom Dad knew, to Sturgeon Lake. Wes and Dorothy were ready and waiting for the young couple, and had a tent set up that they'd covered with poplar saplings, a natural way to keep the summer sun off the tent. Camping was quite an experience for my mom, who was born and raised in the city—even though her family home was on the edge of Winnipeg, where the open tall-grass prairie lay directly behind their street and indoor plumbing was an amenity that still lay in the future. Water was still carried by the bucket from a manually operated pump that served the whole neighbourhood. Winnipeg then was by no means the Winnipeg of today, but it was a far cry from sleeping in a tent surrounded by tethered horses and the Cree Nation at Sturgeon Lake. Dad's new bride was getting a taste of the life that lay ahead of her.

Now that my mother had met Wes and Dorothy at Sturgeon Lake, Dad was eager to take her into Hash Lake and show his trapline to her. On his very next leave, they took the train to Edmonton and then chartered a float plane to take them to the lake. Mom had never flown before and sat nervously chewing gum in the rear seat of the small plane. She repeatedly popped bubbles. The pilot had been listening to this cracking sound and was becoming increasingly concerned, thinking they were experiencing engine trouble. He mentioned this to my dad, who was sitting next to him in the cockpit, and you can imagine his relief when Dad told him what the source of the sound was!

Mom was not impressed with Dad's rough trapping cabin at the outlet. The cabin had never been fancy, but a few years of vacancy had taken its toll: the bark on the unpeeled spruce logs was now peeling off, the roof was leaking, and there were the inevitable rodents. Mom had a toothache, so she lay on the moosehide slung bed while rain dripped onto her through the sod roof and pack rats and mice scampered about. This didn't quite measure up to the romantic picture my dad had painted for her.

Mom's less than positive experience in Dad's old trapping cabin no doubt influenced their decision to make an effort to live the city life for a few years. My sister Linda was born while my dad was still stationed in Rivers, near Winnipeg. I was born in May 1945, when the war ended, and we moved to Winnipeg. We lived with my mom's parents, whom we called Baba and Dedo (the Ukrainian words for grandmother and grandfather), for a short period while my dad worked for Baldry Engineering. While living there, Dad made improvements to my grandparents' house, such as adding a basement. Then we bought and renovated a rambling old two-storey house in another part of the city. Baldry thought my dad had what it took to be a good engineer and offered to put him through university, hoping to erase further thoughts Dad may have had of going back to the Alberta bush. But the wilderness is a powerful magnet, and eventually Dad persuaded Mom to leave her beloved Winnipeg and move back to Barrhead, from where he would be able to spend at least part of the time trapping his old line on the Little Smoky River.

Oil fields were springing up across Alberta in 1951, and it was here that Dad readily found employment to support his young family. He had no fear of heights, so climbing to the top of the oil derricks didn't faze him. This was an exciting new challenge. He enjoyed the excitement of the work, but by the spring of 1952 he'd had enough, and he headed for Hash Lake and the trapline with his younger brother Stan.

The winter had been severe, and even by April snow still lay deep on the ground. My dad and Stan loaded their packs with essentials and enough grub for a week or so away, then tied on their snowshoes and headed for the Little Smoky. The next day, the reluctant spring weather turned very warm and the snow began melting in earnest, causing every creek and the Little Smoky River to overflow their banks. Dad and Stan, camped on a height of land, soon ran out of food, but there was no way they could make it back to Hash Lake or to the cabin on the Little Smoky—they were surrounded by water. There they stayed, comfortably camped on a dry pine ridge, for a solid month, with nothing to eat but beaver meat. Finally the floodwaters receded enough that they were able to make their way to Hash Lake—and food. Stan hasn't eaten beaver since.

Stranded as they were during the flood, Dad and Stan had had plenty of time for thought and talking about the future. Stan had heard that men were needed to work on a dam that was to be built on the Nechako River in central British Columbia. Johnny Hackett, a friend who was a fire ranger, had been through that area of B.C. as part of a government survey, and his reports of the area were favourable. Stan had been born and raised in Barrhead, and had been too young to go away to war and see some of the rest of the world like his older brothers Bert and Bill had. Barrhead was a farming community, and Stan wasn't interested in farming. He wanted a change and needed work to support his young family; B.C. sounded good to him.

Besides Stan's plans to move to B.C., Johnny Hackett's experience of taking a string of pack horses up Cutoff Creek, southwest of Vanderhoof in central British Columbia, spurred Dad's imagination. Coincidentally, Cutoff Creek was in the same area where Alcan, a giant multinational aluminum smelting company, was building the Kenney Dam across the Nechako River. Life in the wilderness that surrounded Hash Lake had been great, but now Dad had a family to support, and the thought of moving to a new place, with new challenges, excited him.

The winds of change were blowing for Wes and Dorothy too. They loved Hash Lake and the surrounding country—"their" country. The land was bountiful and unspoiled and so provided for all their needs. They had no idea that their idyllic wilderness way of life was about to be shattered—till one cold winter day when they heard a strange noise coming from across the lake. An oil company was punching a road in to the lake, and came crashing through near the outlet. That road was like a stake driven through Wes's heart. It was the toe in the door to opening up the area to oil exploration and wells, and like the tentacles of some dreadful monster, the seismic lines and roads spread across their beloved country. Wes and Dorothy could only watch as their Eden was ripped apart and changed forever.

B.C. Bound

Things were pretty simple back in 1953; we loaded all our belongings into the back of our 1949 Ford half-ton pickup and headed for the promised land, British Columbia—Vanderhoof, to be exact. Stan had already moved his young family there and was working on Alcan's massive Kenney Dam project—the biggest earth-filled dam in the world at that time, located 70 miles southwest of Vanderhoof. Dad was confident he could find work in British Columbia and dreamed of buying a trapline there. Mom, who loves apples, was under the impression that the B.C. apples they bought in Alberta stores grew with abandon *everywhere* in British Columbia, so she was game for the move. When school let out in June, we struck off. It was as simple as that. I had just completed grade two, and Linda grade three.

The new Hart Highway through the Pine Pass in the Rockies was a real thrill for prairie folks like us. We'd made many trips across the prairies, between Winnipeg and the rolling countryside around Barrhead, but we'd never before seen mountains—not like the Rockies. We spent so much time looking up at the grandeur of the peaks that we all ended up with stiff necks! The Hart Highway had yet to be paved, but we thought it was wonderful compared to the gumbo of most

Alberta roads at that time. I remember Dad exclaiming that he had the truck up to 40 mph going down some of the hills, and looking over at the big round speedometer on the dash of the pickup confirmed to me the tremendous clip at which we were travelling.

That first night on the road we camped in an abandoned railway shack that teetered precipitously on the edge of a high bank above the raging Parsnip River, swollen to the top of its banks with snowmelt from the mountains. Mom, Linda and I weren't too enthusiastic about this accommodation, but it was right up my dad's alley—it appealed to his sense of adventure. There was even a resident pack rat to make him feel at home. The roar of the river seemed even louder and more threatening at night, as the ground trembled under the little shack. I

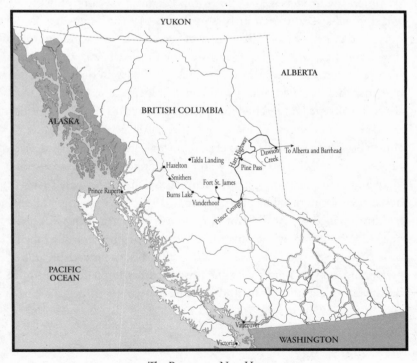

The Route to a New Home

was relieved when morning finally came and we were able to vacate the premises and continue our journey through the spectacular Pine Pass.

Finally we reached the rough-and-tumble, and somehow gritty, town of Prince George; we were on the last leg of our journey as we swung west toward Vanderhoof, the geographic centre of British Columbia. The drive between Prince George and Vanderhoof seemed interminable; it was hot and it seemed the dusty gravel road would drag on forever. We were now on the Interior Plateau, relatively flat terrain, and an endless sea of pine trees passed by our windows as we rolled onward in the midday heat of that early July day. "Where are all the apple trees?" wondered my mom. "When will we get to Vanderhoof?" Linda and I frequently asked. The small paper bag of rock-hard, licorice-flavoured jawbreakers we had bought in Barrhead was almost depleted. We stopped at Bednesti, a little store "in the middle of nowhere," and quenched our thirsts with the luxury of a pop. With the windows rolled down and hot, dry air blowing over our flushed faces, we crested a hill—and there lay the beautiful Nechako Valley, with the small village of Vanderhoof nestled along a ribbon of blue that was the Nechako River. Finally we had reached our promised land. It was July 9, 1953.

The population of Vanderhoof had recently swollen to about 650, almost double the official count of 350 in 1941, mainly due to the influx of men—many with families—who had come to work on the Kenney Dam and then stayed on after the dam was finished. The wide streets of downtown Vanderhoof had been paved in 1951, a new federal building had just opened the April before we arrived, and everything was shiny new and top-notch at the Silver Grill restaurant. The boom from the construction of the dam was clearly over, but Vanderhoof looked pretty impressive compared to the dusty little farming community of Barrhead we had just left behind in Alberta.

Eighteen-year-old Bert on his trapline at Hash Lake, Alberta, in 1937. Note the handmade snowshoes in the foreground.

A group of Cree men travelling with dogs at Hash Lake about 1938. Dogs that aren't hitched to the sled are carrying hefty packs.

Bert's uncle, Wes Reed, hauling hay down Hash Lake in early spring; the dogs are licking meltwater off the ice.

Dorothy Reed could not resist taking this photo, which June called "Halter Breaking the Moose." Bert is on the left, his brother Bill has the switch, and the dead moose is frozen stiff. About 1939 or 1940.

Dorothy Reed poses with a good catch of wolf and marten pelts.

Wes Reed (left) and Bert (centre, in sleeveless shirt) and the rest of the firefighting crew at Atikamic Creek, Alberta.

Bert on Hash Lake in the dugout canoe given to him by an elderly Cree friend.

Two of Bert's dogs hitched to his toboggan, at Hash Lake.

Larry Erickson's dog team and sled, with an overnight catch of
whitefish and tulabee for the dogs.

Artist's conception of Wes Reed -
based on stories by:
Jim Barry

Pen-and-ink sketch sent to Wes and Dorothy by friend Jim Barry.

Sturgeon Lake, August 1944, when Bert was on leave from the RCAF. From left: Wes, Mary, Bert and Dorothy.

Bert with sister Marguerite and young brother Davie in Barrhead.

Bert's parents drove him from Barrhead to Lone Pine, Alberta, in this 1929 Pontiac, shown here having some trouble.

From left: A young Stan, Davie (Bert's kid brother) and David Irvine, Bert's father, in front of their house in Barrhead, Alberta, in 1938. A friend is leaning out the porch window.

Bert is about 20 years old in this photo, which was snapped by a sidewalk photographer in Edmonton, where Bert had gone to sell furs.

Mary Irvine (née Zinko) at 19 or 20 years old, in Winnipeg.

CHAPTER 2

THE ROMANCE OF IT ALL

THEY CALLED THE UPPER NECHAKO HOME

Our first summer in Vanderhoof was glorious, with clear blue skies almost every day—or so it seemed to me, as an eight-year-old girl. We stayed with Stan and Merle and their kids—daughter Patty and twin boys Stanley and David—while we set to exploring the country north of town, fishing its remote lakes. Nahounli was a favourite, and we had great fishing success there. We looked at a trapline the Prince family had for sale in the Fort St. James area, Native Elder Jim Prince accompanying us on the excursion. But my dad wasn't taken with the trapline because it was too close to town, and the surrounding area too settled for his liking. We had so far confined our explorations to the area north of town, and it wasn't until we ventured into the upper Nechako country, southwest of Vanderhoof, that we felt we had found our special place. The rolling country clothed in sweet-scented pine forests, interspersed with poplar and spruce and the open, south-facing side hills, seemed welcoming and friendly. It was as if the country was waiting with open arms, just for us.

The Carrier First Nations, whose well-worn trails future surveyors and settlers would follow, were the first inhabitants of this lovely area to which we were so strongly drawn. Long before white people arrived on the scene, the Carrier had a self-sustaining culture, living off the land and trading with other tribes as far away as the coast—hence the name "grease trail," over which the oily oolichan were carried. Even though the Natives had used this trail for many centuries, it was given the name of Alexander Mackenzie after he travelled this route in 1793. The overgrown depressions in the earth that line the banks of the Nechako in its upper reaches are all that remain of the pit houses and food caches of the Carrier—a reminder that the upper Nechako country was once well used by the Carrier people.

Surveyors Frank Swannell and George Copley began surveying the upper Nechako country in 1908, and the name of many landmarks in the area, including Copley Mountain, Copley Lake and Mt. Swannell, are the result of the years they spent here. Greer Mountain and Greer Creek were named after Tom Greer, one of Swannell's assistants, who was from Pemberton. Many of the early settlers in the Nechako Valley, as well as Natives from the area, were hired by the famous Swannell.

In the early part of the 20th century, and through the two world wars, people of various pursuits were drawn to the gentle beauty and bounty of the upper Nechako. Some were serious homesteaders, while others were draft dodgers, deserters and trappers. These hardy people were sprinkled across the country on the creeks and along the river, or wherever there was a little grass for a few horses or cows. Some, such as the American draft dodgers and Canadian military deserters, were hiding from the law, and their tiny cabins, hidden deep in the timber, gave the impression that they had been built in their chosen locations for sheer survival. Others, who cleared a little land and kept livestock, were obviously making a concerted effort at homesteading.

Most of those who made their way out to their traplines and homesteads did so via Fort Fraser, because at the time it was the main supply centre. Once on the trail to the Greer Valley and the upper Nechako, many spent their first night at the ranch of Bill Erhorn, one of the earliest of the real homesteaders. Bill arrived in the Nechako Valley in 1911, ahead of the railroad's arrival in 1914 and ahead of those who homesteaded and trapped in the Greer Valley and along the upper Nechako River. Born in Wisconsin, he had done a little wheat farming in Washington before heading for the gold fields in Alaska. The rush was pretty well over by the time he got there, so he headed back to B.C. He did some outfitting from Ashcroft and bought four horses, then headed north, thinking he'd like to settle around Smithers. Not finding a place quite to his liking, he started looking around the Nechako Valley, where a Native told him about a big natural meadow that was just off the Greer Valley Trail. Bill rode out to the meadow, and thought it looked pretty good. He set to work carving out a place for himself and worked extremely hard, single-handedly axing out the "cutoff road," which stretched four miles to Tachick Lake, where it took up with the existing wagon road. Twice a year Bill and a friend, George Snell, took a team and wagon over the Telegraph Trail to Quesnel to freight home supplies.

Bill worked alone on his place until the fall of 1927, when he married Hertha Wolf. Hertha had come over from Germany to join her sister, whose husband worked at McLean's sawmill in Fort Fraser. Bill was 47 years old by this time, and what a wonderful change it must have been for him to have a wife working at his side after all those years alone. He'd lived in a shack for many years while he carved out his ranch and hacked ties. Then in about 1920, he built a neat log house set in a grove of pines on a little knoll. Unlike most of the original homesteaders' cabins along the Nechako, this log house has stood the test of time, a monument to a true pioneer family that came and stayed. It was to this cozy home that he brought his new bride. Soon, three strapping boys were born to Bill and Hertha—Bob, Walter and Neal. Bob was born in Fort Fraser with the help of Mrs. Embley, a midwife. Walter and Neal were both born in the log home on their ranch.

In 1913 Bill Erhorn worked at slashing (clearing) the right-of-way for the coming railway, and later he hacked ties for it. When still very young the boys helped limb the lodgepole pine that was used to make the ties, and later, when they reached the age of 16, they cut ties on their own. After the Hobsons bought Rimrock and then River Ranch, Bill and his sons spent time working for Rich Hobson. The winter of 1948–49 was severe, and when a terrible flu hit the country it took Bill with it. Mrs. Erhorn and her oldest son, Bob, were in the hospital at the same time as Bill, both battling pneumonia, but they managed to pull through. Following Bill's death, Bob stayed on at the home place to run the ranch with his mother; Walter and Neal were starting to branch off on their own. Early on, Walter took up land and started his own little ranch south of the home place, and around the same time he also went into the guide-outfitting business with two bases of operation, one at Tatelkuz Lake and the other on the shores of the Nechako Reservoir. In 1948, Neal worked on a government survey in Tweedsmuir Park, travelling with pack horses into the high country, while another crew was working with boats in the flooded valley bottoms. The following summer, Neal and Walter took a string of pack horses up to Coldfish Lake via Fort St. James, for guide-outfitter Tommy Walker. Following these packing expeditions, Neal settled into the hard work of building his own ranch while Walter concentrated on his guiding operation.

Another of the serious homesteaders was Albert Tangdahl, who later changed the family name to Dahl. His brother, Oli, also homesteaded for a time in the Greer Valley, but didn't change his surname. Albert moved to the Greer Valley in 1918, taking up several lush meadows along Greer Creek, a major Nechako River tributary that forms its own broad valley. The Dahl family farmed their Greer Valley Ranch for about 25 years, but when Albert died in 1942, his son, Earl, carried on for only a short time before moving into Vanderhoof to start a taxi service. The Hobsons bought the main portion of the Dahl homestead in 1944 and named it Rimrock Ranch. The Weinhardt family (who will come up again later in this book) also bought their 160 acres from the Dahl family. They would become long-time residents of the upper Nechako country.

Farther up the rough wagon trail, a bachelor named Antoine Nelson settled near the confluence of Greer Creek and the Nechako

River. It was a great choice of location, because another small stream flowed through the property. Antoine had a low log structure near the road from which, according to Rich Hobson, he would shoot at people passing by if he happened to have a gripe with them. This structure was still visible until a few years ago, when the Kenney Dam road was widened to make way for increased logging traffic.

Otto Larson, born in Sweden in 1882, worked for the famous Frank Swannell when he surveyed the Nechako area. Otto had first farmed in drought-stricken Saskatchewan before moving his family to Swanson Creek to build a homestead. The family had a rough start of it. While crossing Greer Creek on their initial move-out, the wagon tipped coming up the steep bank back onto the trail, and all of Mrs. Larson's new dishes were lost in the turbulent waters of the creek. The first cabin Otto built on Swanson Creek, in 1921, burned down after the first year, and life was so tough Mrs. Larson didn't leave the place or see another woman for four years. After about five years of scratching out a meagre existence, Otto and his wife sold out to Rooker White for $500 and moved farther down the river to a location south of Lily Lake, where the Rays, another early pioneer family, had a homestead. The move enabled the Larsons' four children to go to a school that had started up in the area. Larson's Canyon on the Nechako River, near the new homestead, was named after the family.

Otto and Emma Larson had a family of two girls and three boys. The oldest boy, Willie, spent years hiding out in the bush, as he was a deserter from military service during the Second World War. He had several locations where his youngest brother, Hill, could drop off food and other supplies for him. He had a cabin on Lucas Lake and another on a spring above Copley Lake. This well-built cabin was still in excellent shape, shake roof and all, when my dad looked at it in the mid 1950s. It didn't appear to have been used much, so it is possible he built it just before the end of the war. Willie went home to the family homestead from time to time, and on one occasion, when government investigators paid an unannounced visit at suppertime, they noticed an extra plate set at the table—but Willie was nowhere to be found.

Directly across the road from the Nelson place, about a quarter mile into the bush, a deserter had a very small cabin with a shanty roof. His army boots and uniform were still in the cabin when my sister Linda and I discovered it just off the east end of Cathy's Lake. A little farther up the road, Tom Taerum, originally from the François Lake area, trapped and raised cattle at what would later become Hobson's River Ranch. Tom also had a trapping cabin and more land a little past Swanson Creek, where he lived for a time after the Hobsons bought his lower place.

The last places on the south side of the river, and at the very end of the long wagon road from Fort Fraser, were the Hull cabins, located on the river at Cutoff Creek. Hull was an American draft dodger. In size, the large barn he built to shelter his good-looking horses surpassed by far either of his two small cabins. With the exception of the natural meadows that lined the creek, his place was fairly heavily timbered— which leads one to wonder how he made enough hay to winter his good horses. Likely they were just left to rustle along the creek. The buildings were located in a clump of big spruce trees just off the river, not far from Cutoff Creek—fitting, I suppose, since he was a trapper and prospector, not a farmer.

Perched high above the Nechako River, on a cutbank, was the cabin and barn of homesteader Billy Williams. The location afforded him a spectacular view looking down the river—and was well above any floodwater. Located on the north side of the river, he was directly across from Tom Taerum's. Billy cut a wagon road, the remnants of which are still visible today, from his place down to Lily Lake and out to Fort Fraser. Like the other homesteaders, Billy sold out to the Hobsons in the late 1940s.

Interestingly enough, the upper Nechako country was more populated in the first half of the 20th century than it was in the early 1950s. When the Second World War ended, most of the draft dodgers and deserters hiding out from the law simply abandoned the log cabins and barns of these homesteads. Although most of these old cabins are gone now, some were still in fairly good shape when we first ventured into the upper Nechako country in 1953.

THE ROMANCE OF IT ALL

The gypsy life we led that first summer, establishing ourselves in Vanderhoof and exploring the compelling upper Nechako country, was carefree and exciting. However, with thoughts of the inevitable coming of winter and the necessity for Linda and me to go to school in the fall, my dad and mom bought two lots up on the hill on the south side of Vanderhoof. We had a great view of the little town below us, the gleaming white hospital on the other side of the river across the wide valley and the higher plateau and hills reaching northward toward Fort St. James. Our property was the first below the town water tank, and a swath had just been cut up the steep hill, right past our two lots, to enable the hauling of the new tank. Much to our surprise and dismay, one of our two lots turned out to be a freshly excavated gravel pit! (When my dad applied for building lots "up on the hill," he had no reason to believe be would be sold a gravel pit, and the clerk obviously didn't know which lots he'd sold. My dad took this error in good humour.) The other, however, was nicely treed with mature pines and lovely big clumps of birch. It was there that my dad built a one-room cabin that would be our home for our first winter in Vanderhoof.

The cabin was constructed from rough green lumber cut at Oscar Sweder's mill to the west of town. The walls were insulated with shavings, as was common in those days, mainly because there was no shortage of them and they were free for the taking from the planer mill. My mom's womanly touch soon turned the rough little one-room shack into a cozy home, but that winter was a cold one, with temperatures of −40° or colder for extended periods. Despite our wood cookstove, brought with us from Alberta, and an airtight heater that frequently glowed red hot, the inner walls were coated with frost in the many places where the shavings were no doubt a little sparse.

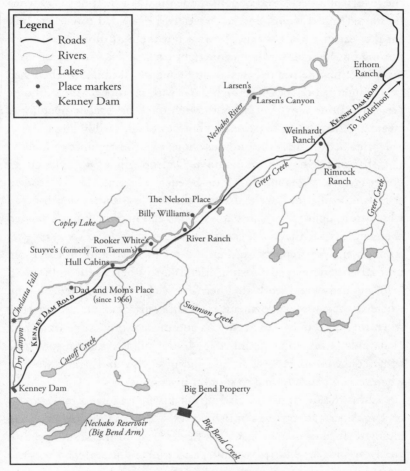

Upper Nechako Country in the Early Days

Of course we had no indoor plumbing. Dad built an outhouse from rough green lumber—including the seat, because we didn't have the luxury of a sleek store-bought model. It was Valentine's Day when he started construction, and so, typically, he decided to cut the hole for the seat in a heart shape. He went out the next morning to finish putting on the roof but then came right back, all excited, saying there was something he wanted to show us. Out we all traipsed. There had been a light fall of snow overnight, and with no roof on the outhouse yet, the pristine snow had fallen through the heart-shaped opening to create a perfect white heart on the bottom of the freshly dug hole—a Valentine delivered via the outhouse hole. Oh, the romance of it all!

That first winter in Vanderhoof, Dad bought a McCullough 33 power saw and did falling for Oscar Sweder; sometimes he also worked at Sweder's small mill west of town. Oscar was a short, swarthy man who bore a slight resemblance to Wes. He and his wife Edie, a slender, energetic lady and the daughter of the Fawcetts, a Nechako Valley pioneer family, were also trappers, so they and my dad had a lot in common. Our families developed a lasting friendship. When Oscar didn't need help, my dad would work at either Mac McDonald's or French's mill, wherever there was employment. He hadn't worried about finding work when we pulled up stakes in Alberta and moved to B.C. He was a jack of all trades—carpenter, plumber, log-house builder, trapper; you name it, he could do it. He was fit and full of energy and would work at whatever job he could find to support his family.

Oscar Sweder took my dad up on his invitation to make a trip back to Alberta to retrieve our two horses, Goldy and Prince, who were biding their time at our Uncle Alan Reed's farm northeast of Barrhead. Goldy was a gentle little bay filly, perfect for my mom, who was not a real horsewoman, although she had done a fair bit of riding since marrying my dad. Prince was quite the character. A solidly built dark bay gelding, he bore a slight resemblance to a mule, with big ears and rusty brown colouring around his nose and eyes. He was friendly and very gentle—a great kids' horse. Back in Alberta, out at Uncle Fred's farm, we'd pile as many kids as could fit on his long, bare back—Linda and me, Carolyn and Jimmy—and off he'd trot, loaded from stem to stern, but not complaining a bit.

After arriving safely in Vanderhoof with the horses, my dad threw up a lean-to shelter for them, digging it into the hillside behind the house. The house was used as part of a fence that enclosed the lean-to, and Prince's favourite pastime was watching us through the windows and mouthing at the verdant plants he could see inside on the windowsills. We had our own little homestead, right there in town. Having livestock in town wasn't that unusual at the time; the Tingleys, just down the road, kept a fair-sized herd of goats that they milked, as did the Floyd Woods family only a few blocks from downtown. Life was simpler then, with fewer rules and restrictions—or maybe the rules were there, but no one paid them much attention. There was room for freedom of spirit, and there was a real sense of optimism in the air.

On our visit back to Hash Lake, Wes gave us some more horses—Cinders, her yearling foal and Tony. Since we had travelled there in a car, this meant another trip back to Alberta to retrieve the horses. My dad's mom, Grandma Bertha, was up visiting from Barrhead at the time, and being of an adventuresome nature, she jumped at the chance to get in on a horse-hauling trip and a little excitement. Cinders was a snotty little grey mare, and Tony a nice-looking bay gelding. Linda had taken a shine to Cinders' foal when we were there visiting, so Wes had given him to her; having a penchant for all things Spanish, she named him Tijuana. Once loaded into the back of the truck and heading for Vanderhoof, Cinders strenuously objected to leaving the only home she'd ever known. Regardless of how short she was tied, she seemed to be able to stretch the rope enough to allow her to get up and pound her hooves on the roof of the truck. The first night on the road, Dad and Grandma stopped at a well-maintained provincial campground just outside Pouce Coupe. The horses were fed and watered and walked around a bit so they could stretch their legs before being tied to some pine trees near the truck. Sometime during the night, my dad heard a ruckus coming from the direction of the picnic table and fumed, "That darn colt's getting into our grub again!" But when he got up to chase the colt away, there was a black bear under the picnic table. He hadn't brought a gun along on the trip, so Dad threw blocks of wood at the bear to chase it off. Well, the bear did retreat, but returned before daybreak, spooking the horses—and Cinders, pulling back with everything she had in her, broke her rope and made a break for it. She was heading home to Hash Lake. Jumping on Tony, my dad set out in the bright light of a full moon, following Cinders' tracks, which headed along a fence skirting the railway's right-of-way. Even though he was able to follow her tracks by moonlight, he decided he'd better go back to camp and wait for morning—partly because Grandma was back there on her own. Soon after daybreak he set out again, giving Tony his head and with Tijuana following loose behind. He came to a railway line cabin where a road crossed the tracks, and it was there, as Cinders was making her break for home, that the horse-savvy attendant managed to catch the wayward mare and tie her up with the only thing he had handy—a bicycle tire. It did the job, so it was back to camp, and with horses reloaded they continued on uneventfully homeward.

Two years after our arrival in Vanderhoof we moved from the little cabin that had become our home to the spacious new log house that my dad built next to it—single-handedly and without the help of any machinery. It was late fall when Mom, Linda and I filled washtubs with moss and chinked between the logs, our hands numb from the icy-cold feather moss. We still didn't have an indoor bathroom or partitions, but we did have cold running water, and the house, with its big windows, seemed palatial in contrast to the dark little cabin. Soon after moving in, my parents threw a housewarming party and invited all the neighbours, including Erling and Alma Gull, Herb and Betty Zeimer, Les and Scotty Halliday and, of course, Stan and Merle. Everyone helped themselves to the beer in the galvanized washtub full of cold water that sat in the middle of the house, and they danced the night away. Our neighbours from just down the hill, the Deans, were from Nova Scotia, and they did some fancy step dancing, something we hadn't seen before. The cabin remained as our guest house, and later Dad's parents lived there for a few years after they made the big move from Barrhead. In fact, that little house held its ground for about 35 years, housing various people, including Mickey and Liz Englehardt and Ed and Georgie Brophy. It was always available for people needing a roof over their heads.

Rimrock and River Ranches

By 1944, Rich Hobson was in the process of leaving his partnership with Pan Phillips and the Frontier Cattle Company in B.C.'s Blackwater and Batnuni country. Wanting a place of their own, he and his wife, Gloria, bought the Dahl place on Greer Creek. Mrs. Dahl had moved to town following her husband Albert's death in 1942, and it was from Mrs. Dahl and her son Earl that they bought the property.

The ranch had been vacant for a few years when the Hobsons bought it, and flooding by Greer Creek, which winds its way through the property before eventually spilling into the Nechako River, had taken its toll on the house and other buildings, washing away the family garbage dump and carrying sheephides into the yard. The place was quite a mess. Soon after cleaning things up, Rich rode back to Batnuni, where he spent the summer riding herd on 500 head of cows and their calves. Trailing the cattle 20 miles up Batnuni Creek to the headwaters of Big Bend Creek and spending the summer there was his last duty for the Frontier Cattle Company. Since he would be away all summer, he hired Sam Goodland to make repairs to the original ranch house on the property and build a log house a little farther back from the creek. When the new house was completed, the old ranch house was used as a bunkhouse for hired help or caretakers.

The volcanic rock wall that projected skyward directly behind the old ranch house inspired Rich and Gloria to name the ranch Rimrock. These rock cliffs were frequently struck by lightning, the violent claps of thunder echoing down the long valley. During the spring of 1956, my family looked after Rimrock for newlyweds Mickey and Liz Engelhart, who had been caretaking the ranch for Rich and Gloria and were away for about a month on their honeymoon. During one particularly violent storm, the kitchen door flew open as Rich's big St. Bernard–Shepherd cross, Boswell, struck the door with his massive front paws, streaked through the kitchen and into the bedroom, where he dove straight under a bed. With the same clap of thunder the oven door on the wood cookstove fell open with a bang, the windows rattled, and we all felt like diving under a bed!

While still at Rimrock, the Hobsons began the process of buying Tom Taerum's place on the Nechako, about 18 miles past Rimrock. They named it River Ranch, because the broad, snaking Nechako River winds its way through the entire property. Following the Greer Creek floods of 1947 and '48 at Rimrock, which destroyed some of the hay and left the land covered in silt, hay was put up on the River Ranch meadows, and in early March 1949, the cattle were moved there to be fed. Over the course of the next few years, Rich and Gloria expanded their new ranch by buying not only Tom Taerum's other place farther up the river, but also the small homesteads of Rooker White, Antoine Nelson and Billy Williams on the other side of the river. In addition to acquiring these old places, Rich took out a pre-emption on the Crown land that lay between River Ranch and the newly acquired upper property of Tom Taerum. The pre-emption tied the properties together, and with the addition of the other homesteads and a further pre-emption across the river, this unique and beautiful holding truly became a river ranch in every sense of the word.

During this time, both Neal and Walter Erhorn, as well as Herman Weinhardt and Sam Goodland, worked for Rich and Gloria at both the Rimrock and River ranches. Walter, at age 16, was one of the crew that in November 1945 took a string of pack horses through to Pan Phillips' Home Ranch to move a herd of cattle to Rimrock. The round trip took them 42 days.

After years of developing both the Rimrock and River ranches concurrently, the Hobsons sold Rimrock in 1957 to Arthur and Grace Brophy, ranchers from South Dakota. The road into Rimrock used to branch off the road to the Weinhardt ranch, the last part winding down a steep hill before crossing the creek. Since Greer Creek frequently flooded in spring, cutting off access to the two houses and barnyard, the Brophys eventually constructed a new road, doing away with the steep approach and the troublesome creek situated at the very bottom of the grade. Years later, one of Arthur and Grace's sons, Jim, and his wife Lyla built a house on higher ground on the north side of Greer Creek, where they didn't have to worry about flooding every spring. Jim and Lyla raised their family on Rimrock and still live there today, operating their successful cattle ranch.

The old house at River Ranch, originally Tom Taerum's home, sits proudly on a hill overlooking the meandering river and fields to the west, with the rocky, angled face of Bungalow Mountain providing a picturesque backdrop for it all. The main part of the house is two storeys, and there is a log lean-to-style section housing the kitchen that Sam Goodland added on. According to my dad, the main part of the house, which appears to be of frame construction, is actually constructed of squared upright logs covered in boards. In the expansive living room, Rich had a homemade barrel heater that Pat Patterson had welded for him. Near the bottom of the heater protruded a big cylindrical draft into which paper was stuffed, and when lit it had a blowtorch-like effect—with good kindling and dry pine firewood, it wouldn't be long before the sides of the heater were red hot and the living room cozy. My dad ended up with that heater, and used it until the sides became so thin from years of hot fires that they buckled and cracked. He then patched it and continued using it for quite a few more years. In the roomy kitchen of the ranch house, a big chrome-trimmed McClary wood cookstove with a warming oven provided the heat to cook many a meal that hit the heavy wood table, rarely without extra guests. The table, with benches along each side, was positioned with one end to the east-facing kitchen window. From there one looked out over the roadway coming up the hill from the barn and the wrangle pasture, where the "wrangle" mare and other horses that were in various stages of training grazed. Rich enjoyed splitting wood, so when he was there he kept the massive, heavy-lidded woodbox full. Located beside the warmth of the cookstove, it was the best and most coveted seat in the house.

The River Ranch house was quite unique; the high wall between the kitchen and the living room was once the outside wall of the original part of the house, the kitchen having been built on by Rich and Sam Goodland shortly after the Hobsons bought the ranch in 1947. High over the door to the living room hung a painting of an elderly grey-haired man with a flowing handlebar moustache and a rifle slung in the crook of his arm. The man in the rustic framed painting, appropriately titled *The Hunter,* kept his watchful eye on the goings-on below in the kitchen. If he ever disapproved, he was never known to fire a shot.

Gloria was fond of robin's-egg blue, a colour she applied to many things, including the corner china cabinet with mirrored back panels just inside the blue kitchen door. The trim around the windows on the outside of the house was painted blue, as were the wooden lawn chairs in the backyard. Robin's-egg blue became Gloria's trademark of sorts; when you saw something painted that colour, you knew she must have had a hand in it.

The Hobsons hired my dad to do extensive renovations to their River Ranch house. A bathroom was plumbed in just off the kitchen in the log section, a bedroom was built on for Rich and Gloria's little daughter, Cathy, and a small office was tucked in under the stairs, just off the living room. It featured a built-in desk below a window with a view to the river. The staircase, which was originally on the outside of the house, was closed in, and yellow fibreglass panels were installed in the roof to let sunlight in. Old family photos graced the wall along the stairs. A sundeck was built over the back patio, with access from upstairs, and a long dormer window, giving an awe-inspiring view of the river valley below, was constructed in the first bedroom off the stairs. The little bedroom on the east end was Gloria's haven.

Gloria was an interior decorator, and her talent turned the renovated old trapper's house into a tastefully decorated home. Thick squares of straw matting were laid wall to wall in the large living room, lending a real warmth; two sets of long, paned windows, with a smaller clear window in between, looked out over sweeping views of the river valley and Bungalow Mountain to the north. The windows were draped in tapestry curtains, embroidered with birds and flowers, and between the two sets of windows a long dark oak table divided the spacious room. In the far corner of the living room was a bed that came in handy when all other beds were taken. Tanned coyote hides hung beside a window on the end wall, near the doorway coming from the kitchen; below the hides sat a chintz-covered couch and rustic pine coffee table that, among other things, Gloria had commissioned Sam Goodland to make. Coal-oil lamps, painted blue, of course, were mounted on the walls. Wicker furniture near the front windows lightened up the decor, and in summer there were always vases filled with fresh bouquets of wildflowers, often picked by Rich's mother, Grizelda. It was a wonderful room, one that Linda and I enjoyed immensely as we sat at the big oak table doing our school work by correspondence during the two winters our family would later live at River Ranch.

CHAPTER 3

TRAPLINE LIFE

A DREAM COME TRUE

In addition to the homestead he had sold to the Hobsons, Tom Taerum also had a place five miles farther up the river. When Tom was ready to move on, he sold this place as well to Rich and Gloria, who in turn sold it to Stuyve Hammersley, an American in his late twenties who was the son of an old friend of Rich's family. Stuyve had a place in Arizona, where he had spent his winters going to university. He kept a few good horses and was independently wealthy as the result of a large inheritance—or so we understood. Word had it that Stuyve was living off the interest from the money he had in the bank. Today this is not uncommon, but in Vanderhoof in the 1950s it was practically unheard of. Stuyve had been to university, but as far as we knew he'd never had a job. Rich knew the Hammersley family from his New York days, and he later named one of his favourite horses Stuyve, after Stuyve Hammersley Sr, our neighbour's father. Rich was Stuyve Jr.'s link to this country. After reading Rich's book *Grass Beyond the Mountains* (1951), and being a bit of a horseman, Stuyve decided he'd like a go at frontier life himself. He wasn't the trapper type, but he bought Tom's Taerum's trapline anyway. I suppose it was the romance of it all: buying a place in the Canadian wilderness and owning a trapline to boot—pretty exciting and quite a change of pace for a guy born with a silver spoon in his mouth and raised in New York City.

As fate would have it, along came my dad, an experienced trapper, and Stuyve agreed to let him trap the line on shares for a year. He and Dad got along well, and the following year Stuyve agreed to sell the trapline to him. Dad was now the proud owner of Tom Taerum's old trapline, covering hundreds of square miles of unspoiled wilderness in the wonderful virgin country up Cutoff Creek and on both sides of the Nechako River. This was a dream come true.

Excited about his new trapline, Dad couldn't wait to show the country it covered to us, his family. The sky was a deep springtime blue as we headed off from River Ranch with our two horses, Goldy and Prince, on that warm Easter Sunday. Since it was the Easter holidays, we were enjoying 10 leisurely days free from school, and our trip would take us to the headwaters of Cutoff Creek. The creek took its name from the ancient Native trail that "cut off" the big bend in the Nechako River and shortened the journey for travellers following the river corridor.

The horses were lethargic in the warm spring sun, and as we wound our way slowly up the hillside out of the river valley, Prince decided this would be a good place to lie down and have a good roll—with me on him. I gave him a few good kicks in the ribs while scolding him roundly, and we were soon on our way again. My mom, Linda and I took turns riding Goldy and Prince, while my dad walked, carrying our entire food supply for the 10-day trip in a small knapsack. He was used to travelling light on the trapline, but the contents of the pack were slim pickings for a family of four. We had left town in a hurry on Good Friday, when all the stores were closed, so we couldn't buy extra groceries; eager to get started on our pack trip, we weren't worried about making do with what little food we had. Our meals consisted mainly of bannock and tea—traditional trapper's fair. My dad was an expert at cooking bannock over the campfire, so it was pretty good, but a steady diet of bannock wore a little thin. We also had the unlikely trail ration of a big bag of brightly coloured candy Easter eggs—not very nutritious, but quite a treat when you're way out in the bush. A few days into the trip my dad shot a beaver, so we had roasted beaver tail to supplement the meagre diet. To cook the beaver tail, we leaned it up against a big rock placed close to the campfire, turning it till the skin crackled and the fatty insides were cooked. Quite a delicacy, especially when you're hungry and tiring of a diet of bannock and tea. This wasn't the time to be picky!

Patches of snow still lay in the bush, but the weather was lovely for April. We revelled in the mature-pine, muskeg-free country, with its kinnikinnick-covered open sidehills, warm in the spring sun. This was virgin country, untouched by humans except for trapping—which, with the exception of the few small cabins that shelter the trapper as he works the line, leaves the land in its natural state. This was an intact wilderness.

Tom's old line cabins along Cutoff Creek had seen better days, and pack rats had taken up residence in most of them, building their messy nests in the stoves and on the beds, their unmistakable scent permeating the dark little cabins. The nests usually consist of an assortment of dried plants (roses are a favourite) and prized items such as cutlery or other shiny objects collected from the cabin. Most nights we opted to make camp under the stars and a sheltering spruce tree, settling down on a bed of spruce boughs, woven together alternately so as to be springy. With the open side of the lean-to facing onto a long campfire, we were cozy as bugs in a rug. My dad rarely used a tent when camping, preferring the old lean-to or wicki-up style for a shelter. Occasionally, back in Alberta in the old days when he needed a base camp for an extended period, he would set up a wall tent with an airtight heater. (In 1938, Wes, my dad and Dad's brother Bill were thus camped when the temperature took a sharp plunge. They were 10 miles south of Hash Lake, in the big timber on Fox Creek, shooting squirrels that were worth a dollar apiece at that time. A thermometer was something they didn't have, but they knew it was darned cold. When Bill's feet froze, they broke camp and headed for home. Back in the cozy cabin at Hash Lake, Dorothy informed them that the temperature at Hash Lake had dropped to –60° F while they were away. She said she had heard on the radio that in Snag, Alaska, a place that was often cited as having the coldest temperature in North America during a cold snap, it had been –80° F.)

We ventured as far as the uppermost cabin on Cutoff Creek, within sight of Cutoff Butte, a prominent volcanic plug used as a landmark by travellers for centuries, before swinging back toward home. Our last night on the trail saw us making camp on a dry knoll overlooking the creek, just upstream from the "firefly cabin," so called because it's set back from the creek on a little beaver swamp frequented by fireflies. The knoll we camped on was one of those wonderful places to be in early springtime, dry and warm because of its southern exposure, the warmth prodding wild onions to poke up here and there from the only partially thawed earth. This was the wilderness country, gentle and bountiful, that we would all grow to love in the happy years ahead.

As we wended our way toward home, we got to thinking about a package of Kraft Dinner we had left in the cupboard. We were looking forward to feasting on this luxury item, a wonderful change from bannock and beaver meat, on our arrival home. Shortly after pulling in, however, company arrived in the form of our nearest neighbours, the Weinhardts, who lived 23 miles to the northeast of us. Bush hospitality prevailed, and, having little else in the house to feed our guests, we served up the precious Kraft Dinner. Little did they realize they were having what to us at that particular point in time would have seemed a gourmet meal. We sat politely by, keeping our guests company while they enjoyed their dinner.

The country we had travelled through over the previous 10 days was a paradise, and we gave no thought to what might lie in store for it in the distant future. Life was simple. Not in our wildest dreams could we have imagined the scale of logging that would hack away at the country until it would become virtually unrecognizable in places, even to my dad, who knows it like the back of his hand.

A QUIET WILDERNESS

By the mid-1950s, the upper Nechako country was very quiet; there were only the Erhorns, Weinhardts, Brophys and us, our family being the farthest out. The Erhorns were about halfway to town, over 30 miles from Stuyve's (where we lived when my dad was trapping), but we still considered them neighbours. Walter Erhorn was like family, and he and my dad would later team up to take clients on wilderness pack trips.

When we spent the winter trapping out of Stuyve's place, the closest family was the Weinhardts, 23 miles away. Herman and Margaret Weinhardt had moved from Saskatchewan to Fort Fraser in 1938, before moving to the upper Nechako country to work for Tom Taerum. Tom also raised cattle, and Herman helped him build a big log barn that stood the test of time until Mark Cramer bought River Ranch and demolished it. Herman and Margaret worked for Tom four years before moving on to work for the Albert Dahl family, whose meadows stretched along Greer Creek. When Rich and Gloria Hobson bought most of the Dahl family's Greer Valley Ranch in 1945, Herman and Margaret worked for them until 1947, at which time they bought 160 acres of meadow land, also from the Dahls. Now Herman and Margaret finally had a place to call their own, and it was on this beautiful farm that they raised their family of four kids— Mike, Ella, Eric and Joannie. When they were of school age, Margaret herded the truck down the road every morning to Laketown, a Native reserve about 15 miles away, from where the kids caught the school bus into Vanderhoof.

One year Linda and I joined the Lakes District 4-H Club, to which the Weinhardt kids belonged. When there was a meeting, my dad would drive Linda and me as far as the Weinhardts and we would travel the rest of the way with them, returning to take advantage of their hospitality for the night. There was an aspect of the Weinhardt house that was unique in our area at that time: it had electric lights. Herman put his machinist skills to work and built a windmill that generated enough electricity to run a few lights, an achievement of which I think he was quite proud, because the lights were always quickly turned on the odd time we were there for a meal, and Herman would sit beaming at the head of the table. Linda and I always bunked with Ella, all three of us in the same bed. Ella's room was upstairs in the old log house and also doubled as the storage room for winter vegetables; a rolling mass of unwashed potatoes and onions had to be navigated in order to reach the bed. Breakfast was always porridge, topped with Margaret's particular brand of homemade cottage cheese. Herman would have whatever was left over from supper the night before on top of his porridge. Linda and I would politely pass on the cottage cheese and leftovers. Life was simple, but good.

Occasionally in the spring Ella would ride her big chestnut gelding, Moonshine, up to Stuyve's for a visit. She'd trained Moonshine herself and was pretty proud of him. We had no means of communication in those days, not even a radiophone, so that meant Ella would arrive unannounced to stay a few days. In my mind's eye, I can see her riding into the yard, beat-up straw cowboy hat on her head, big grin on her face, astride that raw-boned chestnut gelding, still prancing after 23 miles.

Happily, in her later years Ella settled down with life-long friend Neal Erhorn, who over the years had developed a very successful ranch. Ella's newfound happiness was not to last, however. After a rough but adventuresome life, Ella died on April 15, 2000, at the young age of 57. She had been a rancher, trapper, guide-outfitter and, right up to the end, a horse trader, buying horses to sell to the outfitters up north. Ella was a unique character, cut from a different cloth and, seemingly, a different time.

There was one family very near us in the upper Nechako for a short period of time. Bill Edwards set up a small sawmill on Swanson Creek, and he, his wife Wanda and daughter Suzie lived in a one-room, round-topped logging shack on skids. Suzie was about my age, and she became a welcome friend. In spring, I'd ride Wardale, a stove-up old sorrel who had apparently been an army horse in his younger years, bareback the few miles to Swanson Creek. Bill had a nice-looking, high-spirited bay stallion named Foghorn that Suzie rode, and off we'd go together. Several years later, Bill ran into trouble while he was crossing the river, leading Foghorn along behind the boat. Bill told us that instead of giving his horse its head, he stayed the course, and Foghorn drowned. A sad day, and the end of my and Suzie's riding excursions.

Not content to live in Tom Taerum's old log trapping cabin, Stuyve, with my dad's help, built a modern ranch-style house high on the riverbank, looking up a long expanse of the Nechako. The house was even plumbed, and everything was top-notch, including the brick fireplace that graced the living room, thanks to my jack-of-all-trades dad. For the 1950s, this was a pretty fancy house to be found out in the bush, 50 miles from civilization. Stuyve had yet to experience the cold of a central B.C. winter, but once the house was finished he decided he was going to give it a try. Many nights he ate supper with us. Stuyve played the mandolin and was fond of bluegrass music and the classic old ballads, so in the evening after supper, he'd regale us with "The Blue Tail Fly," "Jimmy Crack Corn" and other favourites from his well-thumbed songbook. Stuyve didn't have a bad singing voice, but somehow, in the intimate quarters of our very small kitchen, we felt slightly uncomfortable, even though we knew him well by this time. Maybe it was because he was the millionaire and we were the monetarily poor trappers. Regardless, we were a captive audience.

Linda and I were fascinated by the abandoned log cabins and barns of the old homesteads from times past. When the wanderlust struck after a long snowbound winter, and the thaw miraculously revealed the fragrant brown earth, we would often walk the few miles to Rooker White's old homestead, located on Swanson Creek. His neat little cabin, originally built by the Larson family, was situated on a rise, the back entrance going under the cabin into a cellar. A garden spot was still faintly visible, and there was the usual clump of rhubarb. A good source of vitamin C and in early spring a welcome treat, rhubarb grew alongside most homesteader cabins and even some of the trappers' line cabins. It was usually planted close to the cabin to take advantage of the reflective heat from the spring sun and the water shed from the roof. White's old place fired our imaginations; the furniture in the little cabin was all handmade and still in place, so it was a bit like walking into the house of Goldilocks and the three bears. There were even a few cooking utensils and dishes—the only things missing were bowls of steaming hot porridge on the hand-hewn table. Most cabins on the old homesteads had a screened box affixed to the north wall on the outside of the house; in the absence of refrigeration, this was a place to store food items that needed to be kept cool in the heat of summer. White's cabin was no exception. One day, when we were snooping around and trying to imagine the lives of those who'd lived there, we pulled open the little door on the screened box and, peering in, came face to face with a not so little pack rat. As girls do, we screamed and hastily retreated. That pack rat must have laughed itself silly when it saw the look of horror on our faces.

When Rich's mother, Grizelda—or "Peachy," as she was affectionately known—moved to Vanderhoof from New York City, she bought a big, partly finished, two-storey log house and hired Tommy Smithers to finish it, including the building of a fireplace. She named the beautiful home Frontier House. Rich and Gloria and their young daughter Cathy spent most of their winters with Grizelda in the gracious Frontier House, while Gloria typed up Rich's handwritten manuscripts and worked part time as secretary in George Ogston's real-estate office. They seldom went out to River Ranch in the winter, and as a result, once past the Weinhardts' place, we were the only people in the country. The road not being plowed didn't bother us much since we didn't go to town often anyway; but one particular winter there was a lot of snow, and eventually the road became impassable. Glen Kimball had been hired by Alcan to come out from town in a Bombardier—one of the company's early models of snowmobile, which looked like it had been crossed with a tank—to check on the dam a few times during the winter. As fate would have it, Glen was from Barrhead too, so my dad and mom knew him and his wife, Eileen. Glen would always stop in to visit and have a cup of tea on his way out to the dam. By this time, Linda and I were getting pretty bushed, so although we'd find these visits exciting—a chance of contact with another human!—we'd hide in the bedroom, daring to venture out only just before Glen left. In fact we were so bushed that by spring, when we'd be hunting squirrels along the road, in the rare instances that we heard a vehicle coming, we'd hit the ground, hearts pounding, and lie safely hidden from view behind a clump of trees or a rise in the ground until the vehicle passed. We really didn't care about not going to town—our lives revolved around the natural world, of which we felt part. This was where we belonged.

Linda and I spent every spare minute of our time outside. We had a few of our own traps set, and we'd check them every morning before starting our school work, which we did by correspondence. We ran our trail on snowshoes, and my mom or dad would clock our time; we always tried to beat our previous record. When we wintered at Stuyve's, we had our line set up at the mouth of Cutoff Creek, and one morning we encountered 16 moose on our short route. Some were reluctant to move out of our way because the snow was deep, and the moose had trampled it down along the creek where they were browsing. Winter is about survival, and the moose weren't anxious to go running off through deep snow using up precious energy reserves unnecessarily. On our occasional trips to town we always made a point of counting the moose we saw along the way; they usually tallied around 40. The majority would be on the river flats below River Ranch, which was a real moose wintering ground—or as today's experts call it, "critical habitat."

Tending our trapline, Linda and I were becoming very familiar with the bush and all the creatures that lived there; we felt part of it all, part of nature. It's easy to understand how the Natives who lived in this country before us must have felt when the white men pushed them out of their territories. Like them, and the other trappers who had gone before us, we wandered the country freely, enjoying its beauty and the interconnectedness of all things natural: otters playing and fishing for their dinner in the river; ravens croaking overhead as they scan the earth below for carrion of some sort, maybe a tick-infested moose that didn't make the winter, or a wolf kill; deer feasting on the wild onions that pop up on the south-facing slopes that bare off before anywhere else in spring; moose browsing contentedly on willows and red osier dogwood along the back channels of the river. And the river itself, the ever-present Nechako, beautiful and alive, even in its diminished state, part of the intricate, perfectly connected web of life that makes up an intact wilderness.

The catch on our little trapline usually consisted of weasels and squirrels, but occasionally we got lucky and caught a lynx or a mink. This caused great excitement because it meant more money, but if it was still alive in the trap it meant we had to kill it, and this we dreaded. Neither Linda nor I really had the stomach for trapping. One morning we approached a big spruce tree where we had a trap set, and there was a lynx pacing back and forth, caught by one foot. We always carried a .22 and were getting to be pretty good shots, but knowing we were going to have to shoot that beautiful animal, we felt terrible. It is a demoralizing experience to have to kill an animal that has no chance of escape. The doomed lynx jumped around on the end of the chain and seemed to duck every time we shot, but one of our bullets finally hit its mark. Once the dirty deed was done, self-loathing was set aside and we proudly carried the limp, lifeless body of the lynx, our prize, home to show it off.

Skinning and stretching all our own fur, Linda and I proudly took our catch to George Hawker, a fur buyer in Vanderhoof. George was the proprietor of Hawker's Meat Market, an old-style grocery store and butcher shop with oiled plank floors in the former and sawdust on the floor of the latter. The dim interior of the store was the result of a striped canvas awning that shaded the front window. Mr. Hawker, in his blood-stained white butcher's apron, was serious-minded and always businesslike about our transactions—and I think fairly generous with his payment for our fur. Linda and I entered into these negotiations very seriously, and this was reflected by Mr. Hawker's solemn demeanour.

Years later we were told that he got quite a kick out of us girls bringing our furs in for sale, just like any other old trapper.

My mom had knit me an "Indian sweater," red with rearing horses on the front and back and with a line of diamonds across the top. The sweater, which turned out at least two sizes too big for me, came right down to my knees, and the sleeves had to be rolled up several times. This was my going-to-town jacket, which I proudly wore. Linda wore her old long-fringed buckskin jacket, blood-stained from the squirrels we tied to the fringes for transport when we were on a squirrel-shooting foray. Seeing us like this, lugging our catch of furs in an old gunny sack, George Hawker must have had to work hard at keeping a straight face. Maybe he felt sorry for us, which could have been why he always gave us a good price for our fur—or maybe he admired our self-reliance.

Trapping was hard work, and some winters the catch was very poor, especially during extended cold snaps when the fur "wasn't moving." During those times my dad would come home with an empty pack after two days spent covering his line on snowshoes. We were always waiting anxiously for his return, and our first question was always, "What did you get?" I can remember the sad and disappointed look on his face when he had to tell us that he'd caught nothing. He hated having to return empty-handed. We had no money, so we were disappointed too, but mainly I felt bad for my dad, who was trying so hard. Sometimes, on a moonlit night, he would snowshoe all night because he didn't like leaving us alone too long, especially if it was very cold. When the temperature was −40° or colder—a regular occurrence—the air reverberated with what sounded like the crack of rifle shots, as trees split in the cold. The ice on the river added to the night sounds, booming in protest as it expanded with the dropping mercury. Mom, Linda and I weren't really afraid to stay alone, but we were always relieved to see my dad snowshoeing into the yard. We worried about him too; alone on the trail, any mistake could prove fatal, especially when the temperature hovered around 40 below. There is no room for mistakes when it's that cold. Occasionally, during a prolonged cold snap or a storm, I felt our isolation, and a sense of being very alone and vulnerable crept into our otherwise secure and, for the most part, happy family life in the bush.

In early 1960s, the U.S. Game Department put out a call to its Canadian counterpart, the Fish and Game Department, for live-trapped fisher. The fisher were to be transported to Colorado, Montana and Wyoming, where porcupines had multiplied to the point that they were doing serious damage to the forests (porcupines eat the bark off trees). Fisher prey on porcupines, but there were very few fisher in those states. The fisher is one of the few animals that can kill a porcupine while remaining relatively unscathed itself. To do this, it repeatedly attacks the unarmed face of the porcupine, while avoiding the slashing quilled tail; then, when the porcupine becomes exhausted from trying to defend itself, the fisher flips it over on its back and attacks its unprotected belly.

The call for live-trapped fisher was welcome, because the market price for fisher pelts had dropped significantly. My dad got just $10 for one large male he caught; small females, whose coats were silkier, brought a little more. The local game warden, Art Balcombe, contacted my dad and told him he would receive $107 for each fisher he trapped live and delivered either to him or the Fish and Game Department in Prince George. With the fur market in such a slump, $107 for a live-trapped fisher sounded pretty good.

Some animals go crazy when caged, but the fisher seemed quite accepting of the captivity they endured while awaiting transport, enjoying such treats as carrots, apples and meat. The fisher had to be alive on arrival, or you wouldn't be paid. This hardly seemed fair, since the trapper had worked hard to trap and deliver the animal. However, Dad was quite successful in this new endeavour, and fortunately only one small female didn't survive the trip. It is now mounted and on display at the Royal British Columbia Museum in Victoria.

It's hard for people who aren't familiar with trapping to understand how anyone can trap and kill innocent animals, especially when they have developed such a close bond with the wildlife and the entire natural world that surrounds them, as trappers do. Part of the answer is that fur brings money; trapping is sometimes the only means of making a living in remote country. But that's only a small part of the answer. Trapping is brutal—there's no denying it—but many animals kill other animals in order to survive, and in doing so the balance of nature is maintained. Lynx eat rabbits; coyotes, weasels and most other fur-bearers eat mice; marten eat squirrels and other rodents; wolves kill moose, and what they don't eat themselves, other animals and birds gratefully feed on. Trappers become so familiar with the bush and the ways of animals that they become part of nature and part of its delicate balance, except that they themselves rarely become the prey. Fur-bearing populations are impacted more by loss of habitat than by trapping, providing the trapper doesn't get greedy.

The wilderness, and all that it embodies, gets in the blood; civilization, with all that accompanies it, seems hollow by contrast. Trapping and living in the bush, close to nature, becomes a way of life that's hard to let go. Nowadays, the scale of logging has disrupted the delicate balance of nature (partly due to the mountain pine beetle infestation, but even before that), and for the most part has had a negative impact on trapping. Because of low numbers, trapping fisher is now prohibited, and if caught accidentally in a trap set for pine marten or lynx, fisher must be released if found alive in the trap. The pine marten's preferred habitat is, as its name suggests, mature pine forests, but they also frequent spruce forests; in both habitats, squirrels are a favourite food. But when all the mature pine is either dead or logged, due to the beetle infestation, timber companies intend to zero in on the remaining spruce, and possibly poplar, to fill the void. Culminating in 2005, the licensees involved the public in developing sustainability plans that vow to maintain biodiversity. The B.C. government's biodiversity objectives, however, limit the impact of biodiversity on timber flow to 1.5 percent over the long term and zero percent in the short to mid term, which is considered to be the next 70 years. This they call a "balance" of social, economic and environmental values.

LUXURIES AND TOBOGGAN SLIDE SURPRISES

Our trapline on the upper Nechako River, home during the winter months, was about 50 miles from Vanderhoof. Although well gravelled, the Kenney Dam Road was seldom plowed as far out as we lived, and we had few of civilization's amenities—electricity and phone lines barely extended beyond the boundaries of town. Nonetheless, we were happy and content with what we had, and since there was a road, it was quite a different situation from the isolation my dad had known at Hash Lake. For light, we burned candles, coal-oil lamps and mantled gaslights that hissed as they spread their intense brightness. Our water was dipped by bucket, straight from the Nechako River. Of course, we had no indoor plumbing; it was the old galvanized washtub next to the kitchen stove and an outhouse that was ingeniously suspended on poles that stuck out over a steep bank some distance from the house down a pine-needle-carpeted trail. One small luxury we did have was a radio, a Helicrafter. At night, the radio could pull in almost any station in North America. It was hooked up to a battery that cost $10 to replace, and because of this extreme expense we were limited to listening to the radio for one hour each night. Linda and I especially looked forward to the hour when we could listen to the "Top 10" and sing along—that radio was our only contact with the rest of humanity. The radio was also turned on briefly first thing in the morning and last thing at night to listen to the CBC News, a time I hated because news of the Cold War with Russia scared me. We were directly below a flight path, and quite often at night we heard the distant rumble of jets, oddly out of place in the bush. I often lay huddled in my bed wondering if the Russians were coming to bomb the Kenney Dam or, worse yet, that they already had and the rumble we were hearing was a wall of water, rocks, trees and mud rushing toward us in the cold night. We were the only humans in that quiet wilderness, and the knowledge that we were the first inhabitants below the dam was quietly stored in the back of our minds, though rarely talked about.

Our gas-powered washing machine was another luxury, although one of dubious distinction. With my dad away checking traps much of the time, starting the temperamental beast was up to the women. There was a steel pedal that had to be stomped on hard with your foot to get the motor to turn over—and boy was that pedal polished! After what seemed like hours of the three of us taking turns, the cantankerous machine would sometimes actually decide to start. Whether it started or not, we would be worn out before the work of doing the laundry even began. The washing machine was located in the porch just off the kitchen, and the motor was so loud that any talking was out of the question. It also belched fumes, but if my memory serves me correctly, we had a hose leading from the exhaust pipe to outside. Needless to say, we wore our clothes until they really needed washing, to cut down on the frequency of washdays.

The bank down to the river at Stuyve's was long and steep, which made it tough for jobs such as getting the heavy old Evinrude outboard motor up from the river and into the house for the night—a task that fell to Linda and me. It was also a tough slog carrying buckets of water. But it was perfect for a toboggan slide. There was a trail leading down to the waterhole, cut into the ice, halfway across to the island in the river. The trail wound through the trees and followed the natural curve of the hillside. My dad helped Linda and me build up the curves with boards, which we then packed with snow and sloshed with water, making them icy and fast. The toboggan banked on its edge when we hit these built-up corners, and we gained enough speed that at the bottom of the hill we kept on going, shooting right past the water hole and ending our run just short of the island in the middle of the river. For extra excitement, we sometimes stood up on the toboggan—I guess this was an early form of snowboarding— and pulled hard on the rope so that the curved front came up slightly; ridden this way we were lucky if we made it all the way to the bottom. We also constructed a few jumps along the way. One day my mom came along on her way down for a bucket of water and, mischievous girls that we were, we thought it would be great fun to watch her go down the slide. It took a little coaxing, but she finally agreed to try it, not knowing we had just constructed a big jump near the bottom of the hill, which she'd hit when the toboggan was at top speed. We gave her the big push-off, and away she went. She was doing pretty well until she hit the jump, then off she went in a classic toboggan pileup, landing in a moaning heap. She wasn't amused, and it was then she informed us that she was pregnant, news she had been withholding from us until the right moment. We were stunned; I guess this was the right moment, all right, and we felt pretty bad. Things turned out fine, however, and our brother Dewey was born on September 21, 1957. This was an exciting event since Linda was 13 and I was 11 by the time Dewey was born. We had been a family of four for a long time, working together to get the day's work done. A baby brother was a whole new deal, but something we embraced with enthusiasm.

Of Baby Beavers and Other Creatures

Spring on the trapline meant beaver trapping and shooting; occasionally, when my dad shot a female who looked like she was ready to give birth, he'd perform a Caesarean and bring the live kits home in his packsack. Baby beaver are extremely cute, very affectionate and intelligent. At birth they are about the same size as a domestic kitten and have soft little tails about an inch and a half long. They're born with a good coat of hair, but with their eyes and ears closed. Mom would be filled with dread when she saw the baby beavers coming out of the packsack, because she knew that our rescue effort would probably end in heartbreak; but Linda and I were always up for the challenge. We'd start off feeding them diluted canned or powdered milk with an eyedropper, and we'd wrap them in towels, diaper-like, to take to bed with us at night. If not trussed up in this fashion, giving the kits a sense of security, the poor little orphans cried all night, keeping everyone awake. One morning, to my dismay, the tiny kit I'd been cuddling was dead—I'd obviously rolled over and smothered the poor thing. Most of the beaver we tried to raise died, of what we suspect was pneumonia. The problem was that they were brought into the world prematurely, and their digestive and respiratory systems were no doubt underdeveloped. We always knew when a kit wasn't doing well when it started coughing and bringing the milk back up through its nostrils. It was very sad for us, but we did manage to raise a few to adulthood.

One survivor we very unimaginatively named Beav. He galloped happily around the house, going in and out at his leisure. He loved to come swimming with us, and we had a great time, the only downside being that he had a tendency to want to swim up on our backs, and by this time he was a pretty good size. We contacted Stanley Park in Vancouver and they agreed to take Beav. Looking back, I don't know why we didn't just turn him loose and hope for the best. Unfortunately, Beav was never to make it to Stanley Park; days before he was due to leave for the big city, some visitors arrived with a dog, which attacked and killed him.

Other wild creatures made their way into our lives. Musky was a muskrat that we came upon huddled in the middle of the road, hypothermia setting in; he had obviously strayed too far from his water home. A muskrat normally spends his winter on a frozen lake or swamp, snug in his house. The house has a shelf above the water on which he sits to eat and groom himself, and an opening below the ice to open water and his winter food supply. Musky soon revived in the warmth of the truck cab and seemed to appreciate his rescue. Once home he enjoyed the carrots and other veggies we offered to him in his little cage; we hoped he would eventually become tame enough that we could let him have the run of the house. But I suppose because he was an adult when he came to us, he never became friendly and affectionate like the little beavers. Then Linda and I noticed one day that he had fleas, so we sprinkled him liberally with flea powder, a little of which accidentally got on his carrot, and that was the end of that.

Our menagerie of animals extended beyond baby beaver and Musky, although the others were of the domestic variety. We had horses whose numbers varied from year to year, our dog Rex, and cat Kiwi Darling, and a motley assortment of other animals. All of our animals roamed loose in the yard, and one day our buck rabbit gave the drake Pekin duck a real walloping; he took a chunk right out of him (he survived). Then there was Alice, the orphan lamb that was given to us by the Weinhardts; a ewe had given birth to twins, but she would accept only one of them, so we took Alice home and raised her on a bottle—in the house of course. She moved right in and became part of the family, even travelled with us in the truck, sitting on my lap contentedly chewing on the end of one of my long braids. Eventually Alice became a full-grown sheep and we gave her back to the Weinhardts, who promised she would be used for breeding stock instead of being butchered. Growing up with all these creatures, both domesticated and refugees from the wild, it's no wonder Linda and I developed a close affinity to animals.

After years of Grandma Bertha, my dad's mother, making many trips back and forth from Vanderhoof to Barrhead, she and grandpa finally sold their home in Barrhead and moved to Vanderhoof—"the Hoof," as she liked to call it. Grandpa, a Scotsman who had become accustomed to the prairies, wasn't as impressed with the country as grandma was. He would say, "Nothing but rocks and trees, rocks and trees." He had retired from his job as maintenance man for all the schools in the Barrhead district, and as usual, went along with what made grandma happy. Grandma was a real outdoor person and spent a lot of time with us out on the trapline. She prided herself on having frequent "run-ins" with bears as she walked through the bush, teacup in hand. Thus, one fine spring morning, as she approached the outhouse, she noticed a brown shape moving slowly up the steep riverbank and thought, "Oh boy, I'm going to get a close look at a cow moose!" The cow moose turned out to be a grizzly bear. Grandma headed for the house with the grizzly hot on her heals. Linda and I were out in the yard and heard her yelling, "Bear, bear!" We turned in time to see grandma running as fast as her short legs would carry her with the bear not far behind. Mom was down at the river with Dewey, who was about two at the time, getting a bucket of water. Hearing the yelling, she came running up the steep hill and was aghast at the scene that met her eyes. It was every woman for herself, but somehow we all made it to the safety of the house. Grandma, upon reaching the house, set down her teacup, grabbed a mop and a broom that were leaning against one corner of the porch and rushed back toward the grizzly, waving the implements and yelling, "Shoo, get out of here!" Finally the dogs woke up, and grandma bolted back into the house again. We slammed the door and all rushed to the kitchen window. The grizzly reared up on his hind legs and stood in the middle of the backyard surveying the layout. We watched the scene unfold from the safety of the house, mesmerized, and it was not until the dogs had got the bear on the run that we remembered we had a camera with film in it! But the bear was gone, and grandma put the kettle on to make a fresh cup of tea.

The Brophys were riding in the area the following day, putting their cows out on the range, when they ran into the same bear. He refused to get off the trail when they cracked the long blacksnake whip they always carried. My dad, not wanting a grizzly with a cranky disposition to make a return call on us when he was away, trailed and shot the bear, who was a runt and not in very good condition. After skinning the grizzly, he slung the hide over a sawhorse, where Linda and I had grandma pose with her mop and broom while we took her portrait—though it was not quite the action shot we might have had.

Another run-in with the wildlife that called the Nechako country home took place when my dad and Dewey, who was about seven at the time, took a boat up the reservoir to do some beaver shooting. Prepared to spend a few days, they made camp in a small sheltered cove. During that spring night they heard the blood-curdling cries of cougars in the distance, but it didn't really concern them much; this was the cougar mating season. They were sleeping soundly when, just before daylight, a group of the big felines came screaming through camp, racing past—just feet from their heads—between the lean-to and the dying fire. My dad's rifle was leaning against a tree on the other side of the fire. With the cries of the cougar trailing off in the distance and the grey light of dawn creeping in, my dad grabbed his rifle and started out after them, leaving Dewey at camp. He hadn't gone far when he heard, "Dad, Dad!" Dewey had crawled out of his sleeping bag and was trying to follow. Knowing Dewey wouldn't be able to keep up, my dad abandoned his pursuit of the big cats. There's nothing like an early morning wake-up call.

My dad tells another cougar story this way:

It was in the middle of winter and the snow was deep. I had a trap set across the river, with a moose I'd shot as bait. When I went over to check the trap, I found there'd been a cougar in it. He'd managed to pull his leg out of the trap. We were living at River Ranch that winter and Don Hogarth was staying with us to do some trapping. Anyway, the next morning Don and I crossed the river and snowshoed back to where I had the trap set. The cougar had gone back to the moose carcass, and there he was, lying on a porcupine he'd killed. He saw us and ran before we could get a shot off. We trailed him all that day, backtracking on our snowshoe trail. Don was travelling a little slower, and several times the cougar crossed the trail between us. The next day we went back with three dogs and I trailed it all the way up Copley Mountain—on snowshoes. Don stayed behind. The dogs really wanted to go, so I let them, and all of a sudden they came back. I lost the track for a while, then noticed some broken branches at the bottom of a spruce tree and the dogs were all looking up. There was the cougar. I shot it with my .22 and it came crashing down, almost hitting the dogs. Coming down the mountain, carrying my gun and the big cougar was pretty tricky. One place I started skidding and was heading for a big limby spruce tree, so I let go of my rifle—it flew up in the air and then came down and hit me on the head. When I met up with Don, he saw all the blood on my face and figured I'd tangled with the cougar! We finally made it back to the ranch. Art and Jim Brophy, who'd somehow heard about the cougar, came to see it, and Arthur had his picture taken standing beside it. The girls took pictures of Don and me and Arthur Brophy with the cougar. I skinned it out and took it into Art Balcombe, the game warden. He gave me 20 dollars bounty and said that meant I had to give him the hide. So I did all that for 20 bucks.

Another spring beaver trip was spiced up a bit. My dad had been camping at Copley Lake and had skinned his beaver and then done a little fishing. Smelling of beaver and fish, he was walking through some windfall back to his camp when out of a little swampy area about 50 feet away charged a big black bear. Raising his .22 automatic, the gun he used for shooting beaver, all he could see was black. The scope on the gun had a small field, but he was able to focus on a white spot on the bear's throat, and he fired three shots. The bear turned, and one more shot in its side dropped it not 20 feet from my dad. Too close. He skinned the bear out and packed the hide home, where he stretched it on the outside wall of the barn; we have a photo of a young Dewey pretending to shoot it with his toy gun. Judging from the size of the hide, my dad figured the bear weighed about 400 pounds. That's a good-sized black bear.

A Welcome Guest

While we were busy with our lives on the upper Nechako in the late 1950s, a light came into Wes and Dorothy's lives back in Alberta at Hash Lake. Larry Erickson, an 18-year-old from Edmonton, had heard about Wes and Dorothy through a packer he'd worked for at Sunset House. Thinking he'd like to get to know these people, he wrote to them. Wes and Dorothy enjoyed having company and teaching wilderness skills, so they happily travelled to Edmonton to meet with Larry's family and make arrangements for him to spend a few winters with them at Hash Lake. Larry recalls these days of old with great fondness:

I spent two wonderful winters, 57/58 and 58/59, with Wes and Dorothy, learning trapping, dogs and horses and the lost art of living in the wilderness. They were very taken with and inspired by nature; they were very much in love with their way of life, which required little money. They had a good garden, a lake full of fish and lots of moose meat. They tanned hides to make their own leather, made all their own dog harnesses and sleds. How well I remember so many days and nights camped out with Wes and our dog teams in shelters built with a reflector fire in front; Wes with his big poker stick he always had to keep the fire burning to keep the smoke and cocs [the coals in the fire] from hurting your eyes; the black billycan, moose meat, and bannock and brown sugar for desert. It was a great life. We tanned hides to make rawhide and some of our clothing; we built toboggans. Wes was a great shot and a very good gunsmith; being a sniper in WW I helped to sharpen these skills. Wes pronounced Iosogun [*sic*] "U-saw-gun." They were 70 miles from Whitecourt one way and 70 miles from Sturgeon Lake the other way. Dorothy made the trip out and back in the dead of winter with her dog team, camped out in cold weather on her own—an amazing woman. What little they needed from the outside world was mostly brought in by dog team. They used nine dogs and two toboggans, one behind the other. I learned how to make light and very warm sleeping bags and robes from snowshoe-hare hides, and they told me how wool in its natural, unwashed form was very warm. We trapped the upland fur through the winter and some beaver through December; then towards spring when the snow was mostly gone but the ice was still good on the lake we'd trap muskrats—the lake was full of them. We'd load everything we needed on a big stoneboat-type sled, which you could load everything on because the lake was glare ice and the dogs could pull several times their own weight. We'd circle the lake with traps and check them every other day. When that was over and the lake started to open, the highlight of the season was the spring beaver trapping.

When Larry left Hash Lake in 1959, he travelled to B.C. and bought a trapline and guiding territory at Manson Creek, north of Fort St. James. We were on the trapline and living in our cabin at Stuyve's when he came for a visit. He told us, "Wes and Dorothy were one of the great influences in my life. Without the knowledge I got from them I would never have been able to live the life I have. Wes told me I would end up like many others—in the back-country with a bunch of dogs and horses. That's what I wanted and that's what I did."

The "power toboggan" (early snowmobile prototype) that Bert traded to friend Curtis Buchannan for a horse, Poncho.

Don Hogarth poses with the cougar that Bert trailed and shot. The photo was taken in the kitchen at River Ranch in 1958.

Linda and June hand-feed beaver kits, rescued by Bert via caesarean section.

The hide of the bear that Bert shot in self-defence at Copley Lake is stretched out on the side of the barn. Here, son Dewey pretends to shoot the bear.

Grandma poses, mop and broom in hand, with the hide of the grizzly that chased her from the outhouse.

Having fun posing for a family photo along the banks of the Nechako. From left: Mary, June, Bert (holding Dewey), Linda and Grandma Bertha (Irvine).

Two-year-old Dewey with beaver—this one is frozen—in April 1958.

Dogs harnessed and ready for a trip over the trapline. Wes stands by his toboggan, and to his left is Larry Erickson's dog team.

Eighteen-year-old Russ Westlake, from Curlew, Washington, spent a winter trapping with Bert. They are pictured here with some of their spring catch—beaver and otter pelts.

Russ Westlake and Bert packing out a moose in the late fall. This is how it was done in "the old days," before the advent of the ATV.

Linda, in her early teens, with her first deer; Rex supervises.

Herman and Margaret Weinhardt visiting when the Irvines lived at Stuyve's (1959).

CHAPTER 4

ON THE RIVER

A RIVER DAMNED

Three years before our family became acquainted with the upper Nechako, a change of great magnitude had come to the country and to the river. Neal Erhorn clearly remembers two big pine trees that stood sentinel on either side of the wagon road that led to the upper Nechako country. One branch of the road swung right toward the river, the other left to the Weinhardts' and down into Rimrock Ranch on Greer Creek. Then the giant multinational aluminum smelting company Alcan moved in. Gone were the two big pine trees and the steep ascent to the creek, and in their place was a wide gravel road that from then on would be called the Kenney Dam Road, a road that would see up to 1,500 men, massive trucks and equipment, and tons of supplies hauled over its dusty length during the next few years. The virgin Nechako country had been permanently ripped open, and the quiet solitude of the wilderness had been shattered. A temporary town was established at the Kenney Dam site, and a big camp was set up just this side of Cutoff Creek, on a natural meadow that had a spring providing the camp with good water. A few years later this infrastructure, both at the dam and at Cutoff Creek, was all gone. The only signs that people had once lived on these spots were the discarded items—washing machines and

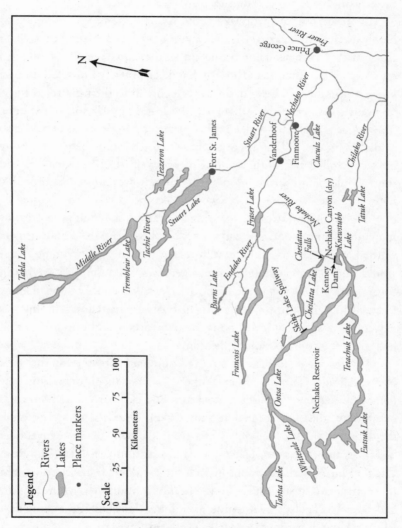

Nechako Watershed and Reservoir

other unwanted household items—that had simply been pushed over the embankment at the dam site.

Because Stan had worked on the Kenney Dam, we learned even before leaving Alberta that Alcan had completed its dam on the Nechako River in 1952, the diversion tunnel under the dam having been plugged on October 8 of that year. The river had been severely impacted, but we knew it no other way. My dad was accustomed to the unfettered rivers he knew in Alberta: the Athabasca, the Little Smoky and the Paddle. These were rivers that flooded in the spring, causing all sorts of havoc, so to dad's way of thinking there might actually be some benefit to living on a controlled river—the volume of water would be predictable and there would be no spring floods. Years later, however, the unseasonably high "summer cooling flows" would become part of the Nechako's flow regime in an attempt to mitigate warm water temperatures for spawning salmon, and my dad's dock on the river would be routinely washed away. Nor could he have foreseen that in years to come Alcan would begin diverting much more water away from the river, so that in spring, when most rivers are high, the Nechako would be too shallow to navigate with the propeller-driven boats he used for trapping. As newcomers, we knew little about the controversy and opposition that had preceded construction of the dam.

A water release facility, although recommended by the International Pacific Salmon Commission and others, was not incorporated into the dam. The Kenney Dam is just a big rock and clay barrier, with no gates or spillway (these are located at Skins Lake). Once the tunnel through the dam was blocked, the only water coming down the wide gravel river bed in its upper reaches, below the dam, was from a few creeks—Rum Cache, Murray, Cutoff, Swanson and, further down, Greer Creek—but these streams were almost dry in the heat of midsummer. Murray Creek had been blocked off by a temporary timber dam built at its outlet on Murray Lake, but some seasonally regulated flow was allowed through for migrating salmon. Below the confluence with the Nautley River, and much farther downstream below the confluence with the Stuart River, the

Nechako was vastly larger because of the large volumes of water these two rivers contributed. For the same reason, these tributaries also provided a temperature-moderating effect on the lower reaches of the Nechako.

The Nechako reservoir was still filling when we arrived in 1953, so water was not yet being released from the spillway at Skins Lake. In the river's upper reaches we could wade from one side to the other almost anywhere we chose, and we did that one day at River Ranch when the Weinhardts came up for a visit. They seemed stunned by what had happened to the river they had known, but we did not understand, being the newcomers who had never seen it any different way. None of us understood the full magnitude of what had happened. We either didn't know or couldn't comprehend that, behind the dam, a whole series of lakes and their vibrant connecting rivers had been ruined by the rising water and would never be the same again. The only waterway in the chain that would retain any semblance of a river was the Redfern Rapids, which connects Eutsuk and Tetachuk Lakes, and the flow of water between Tetachuk Lake and Euchu Reach. As for the Nechako, fish were stranded everywhere in hot pools of water, doomed to die.

Fish were given no consideration when the gates at Skins Lake slammed down. The building of the Kenney Dam, and the subsequent years while the reservoir was filling and Nechako water was completely cut off, took a huge toll on resident fish such as rainbow trout, Dolly Varden, white fish and the now endangered Nechako white sturgeon. Miraculously, thanks to some cool, wet summers, a remnant of the chinook salmon that spawn in the upper Nechako survived to rebuild their population to some degree. The sockeye that travel up the Nechako to spawn in the Stuart system faired better, since they travel only in the part of the river below the confluence with the naturally flowing Stuart. In recent years, however, sockeye have started to show up in the upper reaches of the Nechako.

By the spring of 1957 the reservoir was full, and the pendulum swung in the opposite direction, from near-dry riverbed to near-flood-level water. Alcan began releasing tremendous volumes of water into the

Cheslatta River from the Skins Lake spillway. The Cheslatta had been a very small stream, with an average annual flow of about 175 cubic feet (5 cubic metres) per second, and Murray Creek, with its falls, was only an average-sized creek. Alcan was now releasing massive volumes of water, and this had a devastating impact on both the Cheslatta River and Murray Creek. The torrents raging through these formerly small watercourses gouged a deep channel out of the hillsides and much of the soil from this large-scale erosion was carried through Cheslatta and Murray Lakes and deposited downstream in the Nechako, covering the spawning beds with a layer of silt and compounding the difficulties of the few remaining chinook salmon. For the time being, lack of water was no longer the chinook's problem.

The Nechako turned to mud in 1961, when water volumes of approximately 15,000 cubic feet per second were released from the spillway, the flood of water carving a new path that bypassed Cheslatta Falls. Previous to this disaster, the water in the river had cleared somewhat, and resident fish populations were on the rebound. The river was usable again, there was plenty of water for a propeller-driven boat, and my dad was able to use his boat to trap. But now the river was full of silt and debris because nothing was done about the washout around the falls, and some water continued to take that course. This was a ticking time bomb. In 1972, the river again became thick with silt, and big trees—roots and all—floated past my dad and mom's place below Cheslatta Falls. Knowing that something of great magnitude had taken place, my dad went up to investigate. He saw that the river was running through the channel it had cut when it bypassed the falls in 1961, and a whole hill had now been washed away. Much of the sand, gravel and rock from this washout created the Cheslatta fan, but some of it was carried downstream, and the undulating spawning beds caught some of the silt. It was after this last washout that Alcan built a coffer dam to prevent the water from taking that route again—but they were closing the barn door after the horse had bolted. Alcan was not taken to task for causing this environmental damage to the Nechako

River, but when any suggestion of a change to their legal agreements is made they are always quick to demand compensation or threaten legal action. Alcan's attitude seems to be improving slightly in recent years. Their involvement in the Nechako Watershed Council, and the recovery process for the endangered Nechako white sturgeon, seems to be helping them to see beyond aluminum smelting and power production. But there's always that old bottom line, and I wonder, can a tiger really change its stripes?

"On the River, by the River and for the River"

We loved the upper Nechako country in its entirety, but it was the river itself that would become the focal point around which our lives revolved. From Cheslatta Falls on down, my dad knew every rock and ripple in the Nechako—he was an expert boatman. He built most of his own boats, mainly from lightweight plywood. With his old 22-horsepower "Speedy Twin" Evinrude motor clamped onto the stern, he could make the lightweight boats hydroplane—that is, lift out of the water as they rocketed up and down the river. After one such high-speed trip—my dad deftly manoeuvring between the rocks and with the thin bottom of the boat trembling—Don Hogarth, who guided for my dad for many years, swore he'd never get in a boat with him again.

Like Water Rat in *The Wind in the Willows*, we lived on the river, by the river and for the river. The only mishap of any great magnitude that ever happened to us on the river involved helping the Brophys rescue two of their calves, which had become stranded on the north side of the river late one fall. Winter had already set in with a vengeance and the snow was deep.

The river was high and still open that cold November day when my dad came cruising down with bales of hay in the bow of his boat to meet Arthur, Jim and Ed Brophy. At the spot on the south bank where he had agreed to meet them there was no sign of the Brophys, so he took the boat to the far side, unloaded the hay and rounded up the calves, who hadn't strayed very far in the deep snow. Looking across the river and seeing that the Brophys had arrived, he went back across to pick up Ed and Jim. Arthur, their father, had brought along a 10-foot fibreglass boat and he rowed it over to the other side in case either he or the boat were needed.

Jim and Ed proceeded to rope and hog-tie the big calves, but it took the combined effort of the boys and my dad to get the heavy, struggling animals loaded into the ice-covered bottom of the 16-foot clinker-built boat that my dad was using that day. With everyone eventually in, except Arthur who stayed with the rowboat, they made good progress toward the other side until the boat passed over a shallowly covered gravel bar, and the propeller hit bottom. My dad cut the motor a little too quickly, causing the ice-laden boat to take a nose-dive, throwing men and calves into the water at −20° F. The calves floated on down the river and Jim started swimming for shore. My dad yelled at him to come back and hang onto the boat, which was floating upright a foot or so under the icy water. Jim turned around and headed back, but a few strokes from the boat his strength gave out and he quit swimming. His feet sunk and, to everyone's great relief, touched bottom. Out of breath and numb with cold, he struggled against the current to cover the short distance to the boat and then grabbed on. Sometimes swimming alongside and sometimes wading, the three men managed to guide the water-filled boat to shore—the shore on the north side of the river. Fortunately, Arthur and his little fibreglass boat were still on that side, so while Arthur waited on the bank, my dad rowed the men, one at a time, over to the south side where the pick-up was parked. Having lost his gloves in the dumping, his hands were painfully cold in the frigid air. Gripping the icy oars and rowing back and forth across the wide river became a test of endurance, but eventually everyone was safely on the south shore. Then came the task of plowing through the hip-deep snow to get to Brophy's truck. It wasn't that far, but the shock of the dumping and the supreme effort required to get out of the river, combined with the fact that their clothes had instantly turned to ice once they were out of the water, was almost too much for Ed, who had a weak heart. He was in shock and passed out several times as they struggled through the drifts of snow in an effort to reach the truck. He wanted to give up, but Jim and my dad wouldn't let him. Finally, they made it to the truck and after a bit of encouragement, the motor rumbled to life and they moved off through the single track they had churned out on the way in.

The closest warm place was River Ranch, where Liz and Mickey Engelhart were living in the bunkhouse while caretaking the place. We were trapping out of our cabin up at Stuyve's that winter, but I happened to be at River Ranch keeping Liz and their baby daughter, Dawn, company. Mickey was in the hospital in Vanderhoof having surgery. What a sight those three men were when we opened the door. Ashen-faced and shaking, clothes frozen stiff and encrusted with snow, they looked like they had just stepped off a ship on some doomed Arctic voyage. The icy men headed for the heater and off came their clothes as Liz, a small, cheerful young mother, proceeded to outfit them in whatever she could rustle up; a cute dress for my dad, her housecoat for Jim and lucky Ed got Mickey's housecoat. No doubt Liz was having some fun with a bad situation!

None of the men suffered any lasting ill effects from the dumping, and in fact Jim, who had a cold at the time, claimed it cleared up immediately! As for the calves, they managed to struggle free of the ropes—which loosened when they became wet—and they were later retrieved from a sandbar further down the river. The boat didn't fare as well. My dad left it on shore with the intention of going back in a day or so when the weather warmed up a little. But instead of warming up, the temperature plunged to about −30° F. Big ice flows moving down the river tore one side of the boat off and swept the motor out into the river. Weeks later he was able to retrieve the motor from the river bottom, but the boat was not repairable. The whole episode came close to being a disaster with tragic loss of life. It was an experience none of them ever wanted to repeat, but none of them would ever forget.

CHAPTER 5

HORSE TALES

A HORSE-FEEDING CONTRACT

In the winter of 1957/58, when I was 14 and Linda was 15, Rich commissioned the two of us—put us "on the payroll," as he liked to say—to feed his 40 or so head of horses at River Ranch, where our family was living while caretaking the place and trapping. That made us feel pretty important, and we took our new job very seriously—so much so in fact that we didn't go to town once that winter.

Rich had had the log barn, built by Tom Taerum and Herman Weinhardt, renovated with a new plank floor and sturdy box stalls. Linda and I swept that floor—keeping it immaculate—far beyond what was necessary. The floor in the loft consisted of loose poles that rolled when we walked on them to get hay—we had to be careful or we'd fall right through.

Rich had a big load of hay trucked in from the Peace River, and the heavy alfalfa-laden bales were bound with thick baling wire that was hard to get off. It took our combined strength to push the bales out of the loft and into the outdoor feeding area, but that was only the beginning of the fun. When we fed the horses, Bugs, a wacky carriage-type horse, would be running with her long stride around the perimeter of the herd, snow flying, while the head honchos would be defending the turf closest to the hay. There was always a lot of kicking, bared teeth and flattened ears as horses lower on the pecking order vied for a position. A spring behind the barn had a small wooden trough to catch the water, making it easy for the horses to get a drink. If it was cold we had to chop through the ice on the surface, but that was easier than carrying water in by the bucket—which we sometimes had to do. Feeding and caring for 40 horses wasn't an easy job for two girls, but we loved it. We knew every horse by name; Jughead, a black gelding with a rather large head who wasn't the brightest horse in the herd; the Peterson mare; Roany, a red roan; the Blue Mare; Rusty, and the ensuing Rusty Jr.; the Wrangle Mare, so called because she was a dependable horse who was kept ready to use in the wrangle pasture; Spud and Whisky, a pair of untrained part-workhorse geldings; It, a rather pathetic-looking animal, so named by Don Hogarth, who was responsible for naming many of the horses; and Stuyve, the old horse that Rich had brought with him from Batnuni. And of course there was Rich's prize Arabian stallion, Lurif, who spent most of his time in a spacious box stall in the barn, getting special treatment. But our favourite was a dark bay gelding named Tex, a well-trained cow horse with a wonderfully smooth gait. He wasn't a bucker but was always raring to go, and needed an experienced rider. His only weakness was that he was rather hard-mouthed, and if allowed to run flat out, he could be hard to stop. There was always a colt or two who no one got around to gelding for a few years, so as well as foals from those mares intentionally bred to Lurif, with spring came a whole new crop of colts of varied origin. We separated the mares from their yearling foals to wean them in preparation for these new arrivals—a rather stressful exercise for both humans and horses.

Linda and I were paid the princely sum of $40 for our winter's efforts, quite a chunk of money to us in those days. Linda used her $20 share of the bonanza as the down payment on a beautiful saddle owned by Dr. Dietrich, a Californian friend of the Hobsons who had bought Antoine Nelson's place. Close to 50 years later, she still has that pretty saddle. I, on the other hand, must have frittered my share of the money away, because I can't remember what I spent it on.

ON THIN ICE

My dad's herd of about 10 horses ranged on both sides of the river in summer, but usually spent the early part of winter rustling (pawing through the snow to get at the grass beneath) through the wild meadows on the north side of the river. If conditions are good, horses do very well feeding this way and actually prefer it to being fed hay—it's less boring, and they have their freedom. Sometimes after being brought in they'll leave their hay and try to head back to their rustling grounds—a maddening situation after going to the effort of bringing them in. After my dad took out an agricultural lease on 250 acres of grassy country along Big Bend Creek, he would sometimes move the horses there to rustle. In those days the "Big Bend" was accessible only by water—the Nechako reservoir—or through some pretty rough country on foot or by horseback. My dad would check on the horses periodically, and when the snow got too deep or the horses weren't doing well, he'd bring them home to feed for the rest of the winter. Sometimes the trip home was a little tricky.

One particular winter in the early 1960s, Russ Westlake, an 18-year-old from Curlew, Washington, was spending the winter trapping with my dad. They'd been in to check on the horses and found them in poor shape, and two had met with misfortune. One had gone through the ice on the lake and drowned, and another was found dead in the creek. The snow was too deep to even think about trailing the surviving horses out, especially in their condition, and the reservoir had flooded, leaving much of it covered in glare ice that was also treacherously thin. But there was no other option; the horses had to be brought out over the ice. Undaunted, my dad fired up "Luigi," our old two-ton truck, and loaded it with the tractor, hay, chopped oats ("chop") and halters as well as camping gear and food; this was probably going to be more than a one-day job. A flatbed trailer was fashioned by fastening some planks to a pair of wheels and a chassis; this was towed behind the truck, and thus they proceeded, crossing the Kenney Dam and then around the corner to a landing. Here, they unloaded the tractor, to which they hooked the trailer loaded with hay, oats, equipment and supplies. Now they were ready for the nerve-wracking drive across the ice to Jamieson Landing, the bay where Alcan had built a cofferdam while the reservoir was filling.

The ice cracked and groaned under the weight of the truck and the tractor pulling the trailer, but they crept on and arrived intact at their destination, Jamieson Landing, where they parked old Luigi. They carried on with the tractor and trailer to the mouth of Big Bend Creek where they made camp, erecting the usual wicki-up shelter and building a blazing fire in front of its open side. They would snowshoe into the meadows the following day and locate the horses, feeding them the chop for a pick-me-up before trailing them through the belly-deep snow to their camp at the edge of the ice-covered lake. The plan was to feed oats and hay to the horses for a day or so to strengthen them before starting the long walk across the ice to Jamieson Landing and the truck.

The next few days dawned clear and cold, but what they needed was snow to cover the ice. Ice strikes fear into a horse's heart—hooves weren't made for walking on ice, and a fall could spell a broken leg and certain death. Horses seem instinctively to know this.

It wasn't hard to locate the motley herd where they'd pawed down a big area in their search for nourishing grass, and they made no effort to avoid the ropes and halters. It was tough slogging through the deep snow, so once at camp the horses were happy to hang around eating hay for a few days, enjoying the campfire and the human companionship. But then it was time to move out—onto the ice. Each horse got another feed of chop and then, carrying the remainder in a sack, my dad started off, leading Goldy, the old matriarch of the herd. Knowing there was chop in the sack and seeing Goldy walking out onto the ice, the rest of the horses decided to give it a try. Snorting and blowing, and with noses to the ice, they cautiously moved away from the snag-infested shoreline.

The water level in the reservoir had dropped, so now there was a deep well with open water around the base of each snag, the weight of the horses causing the loose snags to ominously bob up and down in the frigid water. This added to the horses' apprehension, telling them that this was not a good place to be. Deciding that the best line of attack was to head directly across to Pig Island and then on to its more shaded north-facing shore—where there was some snow on the ice to give the horses better footing—my dad struck off, with Russ and the other eight horses following. They would follow the north shore till they were opposite Jamieson Landing, but at that point they would have no choice but to strike off across the ice again.

The strategy worked as well as could be hoped for, but not without horses going down; several times a horse's feet went out from under him and there he'd lie, paralyzed with fear until helped up on his trembling legs by my dad and Russ, pulling with all they had on ropes. It was by sheer will and brute strength that the weary group eventually reached the truck at Jamieson Landing. The horses were spent after their tense trek across the ice, and were clearly relieved to reach terra firma again. But now all nine of them were loaded into the back of the two-ton truck, and the nerve-wracking drive over the thin, glare ice back to the other side of the dam began. Who knows if the horses sensed just how dangerous this situation was, but certainly Russ and my dad knew. The ice was just thick enough to hold the truck loaded to capacity with horses—so long as they kept moving—and it cracked and protested loudly as they rolled cautiously along. When they finally pulled off the reservoir and rolled for home, the collective sigh of relief that went up from men and horses alike was no doubt heard for miles around.

Chapter 6

THE GUIDE-OUTFITTING ERA

The Heyday of Guiding

Since 1913, hunters who are not residents of B.C. have been required to retain the services of a licensed guide when hunting in the province. Each guide was given a specific area in which to operate—his registered guiding territory. In 1954, Rich Hobson held a Class A Guiding Licence, but he wasn't using his territory, so was in danger of losing it. To prevent this from happening, my dad started guiding as a Class B guide, under Rich's licence, it being mandatory in those days for anyone without previous guiding experience to guide under the sponsorship of a Class A guide. After dad had done this for a few years, Rich—whose time was being occupied with writing *Nothing Too Good for a Cowboy*—was happy for the game warden, Art Balcombe, to reassign the territory to my dad in his own name. The territory was one of the largest in B.C., covering several hundred square miles. It extended from Nulki and Tachick lakes in the northeast to the narrows on the Nechako reservoir in the southwest, and it covered both sides of the river, taking in Copley, Hallett and Bungalow lakes on the north side. Thus began a long career in the guiding industry for our family. The Cheslatta Lake guiding territory was later bought from Jim Clark, and Hill Larsen signed over his territory to my dad, feeling he could trust him with its management. Hill's territory was further down the river, on the north side, bordering Ray's on Hallett Lake; he had cabins on both Hallett and Triangle lakes.

September 21, 1957, was a banner day for my dad; his first son, Dewey, was born, and his first hunting client got a moose—though it's been said that it was debatable which event he was more excited about! His first hunting "party" was Charlie Angelo and his friend Dewey Johnson, from California. (My brother's real name is Mark, but we've always called him Dewey—though the nickname has no connection with Dewey Johnson.) Charlie was a generous sort and brought all sorts of treats with him, including a big paper bag full of candy for Linda and me. We were totally unaccustomed to such extravagance, especially when there was no special occasion to justify it. This was like Christmas! At the end of the guiding season we had money—more than we'd had all at once in years—and my mom took Linda and me into a little store in Vanderhoof, Jeannette's, and bought us each a new pair of woollen gloves, a much-appreciated gift. This guiding business was all right!

The Hull cabins were on Stuyve's property, but they were also on my dad's trapline and guiding territory, and since they were well built and in reasonably good condition, Dad decided (with Stuyve's agreement) to replace the floors, fix the roofs and use them as his base for the guiding operations. The two log cabins faced one another across an opening of about a hundred yards, and were back from the river about the same distance, in a stand of big spruce trees. The cabin closest to the river was the bigger of the two, so it was used for eating and sleeping; the smaller, windowless cabin was used as an extra bunk house and for storage. The road into the cabins turned into a quagmire when the fall was wet, and many times Dad's rugged little four-wheel-drive vehicle, an International Scout, had to be winched out of bog holes the size of small lakes.

Dad has some good memories of time spent in the Hull cabins—though some events are probably funnier in retrospect than they were at the time. One night, after a long hunt, the guys were all bedded down for the night. Short one bed, a hunter had made a place for himself on top of the table in the middle of the cabin and was sound asleep. My dad wasn't sleeping, though—he'd been listening to scuffling sounds somewhere in the cabin and was wide awake, shining his flashlight in the direction of the sounds. Suddenly there was a loud bang and a dead pack rat fell off a beam and onto the guy sleeping on the table. All the hunters were now sitting bolt upright in their sleeping bags, muttering things like, "What the Hell?" From his bed, "Dead-eye" Bert said, "Well, we didn't want him to get away, did we?" They all agreed—except for the hunter who got hit with the bloody pack rat.

My dad took pride in getting the hunters into shape, especially if they arrived soft and a little overweight. He'd walk the legs off them, saying, "This isn't just a hunting camp, it's a fitness camp!" When asked how far it was into a certain destination, he'd say, "just a few miles," or some other underestimation of the distance. Hence the term "Bert's miles" came into use. The hunters usually took this in good humour, and would be pretty proud of themselves as they took their belts in another notch and then headed home to their wives in much better condition than when they'd left.

Well known around Vanderhoof, my dad left his business cards at several of the local stores—and of course the Reid Hotel, the main watering hole. One day he noticed the letters MT had been written after his name on every card at each place he'd left a supply. It looked like he had a degree in something or other. Wondering what it meant—and who had done it—his friend Harvey Reeves, who owned the Vanderhoof Department Store, finally fessed up, informing him that MT stood for "Mad Trapper."

As with any business, the guiding started out slowly, with only a few hunting parties, and for the first couple of years my dad was able to handle the business on his own. But by the late 1950s a clientele had built up and it became necessary to hire extra guides, and sometimes a cook. Don Hogarth, a cowboy who worked for Rich at River Ranch, was one of the first assistant guides hired. Don had started working for Rich at Rimrock Ranch when he was only 18, riding his horse all the way out from the family farm in Prairiedale, 9 miles north of Vanderhoof. He'd become acquainted with the Hobsons by splitting wood for Rich's mother, Grizelda, at her Frontier House in Vanderhoof. Don was, and still is, a wonderful horseman, so he did a lot of the wrangling and packing in the years he guided for my dad. Horses were sometimes used on the hunts, but more often they walked or went in boats. Some of our clients had no riding experience but nonetheless insisted on riding anyway; they'd hang onto the horn, and their lack of balance resulted in a sideways list that made the saddle slip. No matter how many times the cinch was tightened, the rider would end up either on the side of the horse, hanging on for dear life, or under its belly. At least two hunters, including Dewey Johnson and Dale Schmidt, broke ribs falling off, which made the rest of the hunt pretty uncomfortable for them. Horses were often used to pack the meat out and we had about six that were good pack horses; Dixie, Sandy, Tijuana and Goldy were the best. Don always rode and led the pack horse, but my dad preferred to walk and lead the horse—I guess old habits die hard.

Windfall and horses don't mix, so when a moose was shot in an area with much windfall on the ground, horses weren't usually used. My dad and the guides would pack the meat out on their backs, each man carrying a whole quarter, weighing between 125 pounds for a front quarter or 150 pounds for a hind. Although the front quarter is lighter, it's more awkward to carry because of the way the leg pokes out. Sometimes the more fit hunters helped pack the meat out themselves. Upon first encounter, clients often commented on my dad's slight build—they expected a big-game guide to look like Paul Bunyan. They were often amazed at how strong Dad was for his size, and that he was able to carry a whole quarter of moose meat on his back over a rough trail.

On occasion, meat had to be left for a day while the horses were brought in, but bear never bothered it—according to my dad, "they don't like 'hot' meat" (anything freshly killed), preferring to let it "ripen" for a few days. Sometimes a bear would tear down the wrapped quarters from the hanging pole—but they wouldn't eat the meat. One night at the Big Bend, my dad volunteered to stay behind with a moose that Charlie Angelo and Dewey Johnson had shot, while Lorne Bolen went out for the horses. There had been a big forest fire the previous summer, originating at Cutoff Butte, and a Cat road, the route for which my dad and Oscar Sweder had walked and blazed, had been pushed through from Tatuk Lake to aid the firefighters. It joined up with the road (not much more than an overgrown trail by then) to Jamieson Landing that Alcan had built during the dam construction. This meant that for the first time horses could be brought in by truck, rather than over the long trail. When Lorne left to get the horses, my dad set up his usual wicki-up, covering some poles with a tarp, got a fire going and settled in for the night. The wind was blowing hard, and as the night progressed, it turned into a steady roar. Getting up at first light, Dad was surprised to see that the meat had been knocked down and the moose's head was missing. Taking a quick look around for signs, it didn't take him long to find tracks—grizzly tracks. The wind roaring through the trees had blocked out all other sound and had enabled the grizzly to carry out his heist while my dad slept like a baby. The bear probably buried the head and left it for a few days before going back to dig it up and eat it.

Uncle Stan became a regular guide for many years, and he has some stories to tell. Other guides included Stan's son Stanley, Pat Haggerty, Craig Forfar, Jimmy Ray, Lloyd Sjodin, Lorne Bolen and Bud Olsen; even my husband Denis took time off from his job for a few years to try his hand at guiding. Curtis Buchanan, who was also part of the scene, was a good friend of my dad's. One night, in town, he and Dad got to partying at the Reid Hotel and ended up spending the next several days rounding up Curtis's far-flung herd of horses near his ranch in the upper Mud River country. Tony Evans, another cowboy who worked for Rich, was also in on the roundup. Mom was understandably unhappy about this little escapade, as Dad had failed to inform her of his impending absence.

The property that the Hull cabins were on wasn't deeded when Hull lived there, but eventually Stuyve was able to buy the land from the Crown and decided he didn't want the cabins to be used for the guiding operation any longer. He trenched Cutoff Creek to prevent it from flooding the natural meadows, wanting this land to contribute to his goal of a working ranch. My dad didn't want hunters coming in from outside and using the cabins, so he burned them down. It was a sad day, but everything has its time, and change is often for the best. In this case, it spurred my dad to build his own new place, a 30-by-30-foot lodge, further up the river.

A typical hunt in the 1960s, by then at the new lodge, would see eight hunters in camp at one time. With a 4:00 a.m. or earlier rising time, the schedule was gruelling and took a lot of planning on Dad's part, including determining where each assistant guide was to take his hunters and keeping track of all that was going on, while at the same time guiding a group of hunters himself. Lunches were made in the morning and knapsacks packed; if horses were to be used that day, they had to be readied. Once Linda and I had flown the coop and Dewey was of school age, he and my mom lived in our house in town, only coming out at weekends. This meant my dad had to do most of the cooking on top of his other duties, although some of the other guides pitched in, and in some seasons Jimmy Ray, Leo Sjodin or Mrs. Butterfield were hired as cooks.

The evening before the hunt, the hunters and their guides were paired up and taken to the gun range to adjust the sights on their rifles—the target practice often turning into a bit of a competition to see who was the best marksman. Later that night Dad would mull over where the moose were likely to be found, and in the morning he'd tell each guide where to take his hunters, leaving the toughest spot for himself. Before each new hunt began, Dad went over the rules, making sure the hunters understood that they weren't to have a shell in the breach of the gun until they were given the green light to load up and shoot, and they weren't to shoot until the animal could be clearly seen. This precaution prevented trigger-happy hunters from shooting something they weren't supposed to, like a cow moose out of season or a mother bear with cubs. It also reduced the likelihood of animals being wounded rather than killed, though occasionally this did happen and the wounded animal had to be tracked down. My dad never gave up on a wounded animal, always tracking it till it was found and putting it out of its misery.

In the early days—the 1950s to 1970s—tent camps were set up at several locations, one of which was at the narrows halfway along the reservoir, another between Cheslatta and Murray lakes, and one at Hooter Lake. Often, camp was made wherever the day's hunt ended. The location at the narrows was, of course, accessed by boat. One day when the lake was exceptionally rough, my dad had left camp with one of the hunters and had gone only about a quarter of a mile up the lake when he realized it was too rough to go any further—the waves were four feet high and the hull of the 27-foot boat was slamming down hard as it came off each wave. Heading in to shore and cutting the motors, he attempted to pole his way through the deadheads that clogged the shoreline. Seeing that this was a hopeless battle, he manoeuvred the boat back out into open water and headed back for camp. What became evident once they got going was that the wooden boat had smashed down on a snag that had punched a sizable hole in the hull. With the hunter pressing his hand over the hole and my dad at the helm with both motors (one of 22 hp and one of 30) at full throttle, they roared back to camp, where the rest of the hunters and six guides were anxiously waiting. The boat was full of water when they got there. My dad happened to have some bathtub caulking in his tool kit and, once safely ashore, he used this to patch the hole, then tore a board "that wasn't needed" off the boat and braced it in place with a stick. The weather had calmed down a little by this time, so they decided to break camp and head back to Jamieson Landing. Craig Forfar, one of the guides, sat up front, leaning forward, his eyes fixed on the patched hole all the way back.

Many of my dad and mom's hunters came back year after year. Sam May, an ex-U.S. Army colonel from Post Falls, Idaho, was one of them. Mom relates a story:

Sam was in his seventies when he first started coming, bringing along his son-in-law Larry and a couple of other guys, all from Post Falls, Idaho. They always drove "straight through" in one day. Sam was in good shape for his age and he was a good shot, almost always getting his moose. Sam's behaviour reflected the many years he'd spent in the army—he was still the "general," dispensing orders to everyone. Bert and Sam were always trying to get a rise out of one another. One year Sam brought up a really nice pair of boots. Bert had been admiring them. Sam decided he'd better hide his boots at the end of each day. One morning he couldn't find them and there was quite a kerfuffle—till Bert produced the boots, saying that Sam had forgotten where he hid them. Sam would start organizing his hunting party for the next season as soon as he got home. He continued coming till he was in his nineties. When he finally made his last hunt, Sam gave Bert his skinning knife and meat saw as a memento of their many hunts together.

"Big Ick" was quite a character and came for many years, bringing his wife Lil and their daughter, and sometimes other hunters, with him. Ick was 6 feet 3 inches and weighed around 300 pounds, giving the guides incentive to poke fun at him (though always good-naturedly) by getting into a pair of his pants, one in each leg. Ick and Lil owned a pub back in Oregon, and brought up fluorescent-coloured jackets with "Markum Inn" emblazoned across the back, as gifts for all the guides. They never wore out and there are still a few around.

It was during this heyday of guiding, in the fall of 1963, that my parent's youngest son, Rick, was born. Linda and I had returned to school in Vanderhoof, and had both graduated from high school that spring. So as we were getting ready to leave the nest, Dad and Mom had a young family of two boys to keep them busy and youthful.

THE STRONG SILENT TYPE

For a few summers starting in 1959 Walter Erhorn and my dad teamed up to take clients on pack trips. They explored the Sutherland River Valley area to the north, recommended to them by Rich and Gloria Hobson, who had travelled up the Sutherland with horses on their honeymoon. Walter and my dad found the country to be pretty rough, and didn't think it was the place to take clients from the city. They decided that the country south of the Big Bend, up the Euchineko River valley with its open, grassy side-hills, was much more pleasant and suitable. The Hobsons had lined up a family from New York City, the Rosens, and their friends the Weisels, for the first pack trip. "Wee Willy" Weisel, apparently a Count of somewhere, and his wife Carmen, bailed out on the first day—Don Hogarth was tasked with escorting them back to Vanderhoof. That left the Rosen family, Walter and my dad. The expedition into the untracked Euchineko country was to begin at our property on Big Bend Creek, where the horses would be held in preparation for the month-long trip. Linda and I had been keeping two horses for pleasure-riding in a pasture near town, and since they were well broken they would be needed for the two teenaged Rosen girls. This meant we had to get the horses to the Big Bend. To that end, Linda and I rode out to Walter's, some 20 miles from Vanderhoof on the Kenney Dam road, to rendezvous with Walter and his string of horses. There was never a thought that the horses be trucked as far as River Ranch—another 20 miles further on—from where we'd be leaving the next morning. Travelling at a brisk trot, we made good time, but the skies opened up in a typical summer cloudburst as we neared the ranch. The rain funnelled off the rolled-up brim of Walter's straw cowboy hat like an overflowing eaves trough, but there was no suggestion that we stop and take cover from the deluge. Walter was the strong, silent type. A shy bachelor in his early thirties, he was feeling a little uncomfortable in the company of two teenaged girls.

There was no time to waste, and no time for us or our horses to rest up the following day after our 40-mile ride; we'd be moving out in the early morning. The plan was that my dad would go on ahead by boat across the reservoir to the Big Bend. There he'd build a corral on the natural meadow that follows Big Bend Creek, and all would be ready for our arrival with the string of horses. In a few days my dad would repeat the boat trip and bring in the Rosen family, Axel and Kathleen and their two teenaged daughters, who would have flown in to Prince George from New York City to begin their much anticipated, month-long pack trip.

There was no trail to the Big Bend, but this was my dad's trapline and guiding territory, and as for the route that we planned to take—well, he'd been "through there" a few times. That night, as we huddled around the coal-oil lamp on the kitchen table, Walter and Dad discussed the route we should take. The trail to the Big Bend was rough but manageable—no big deal.

Walter, Linda and I set out early the next morning under the clear blue skies of July, each of us leading two horses. Making good progress through the open pine country of upper Cutoff Creek, we stopped on a knoll to have some lunch and rest the horses. I don't remember if Walter said something like "We'll stop here for lunch" or if he just stopped and started unsaddling his horse. I think it was the latter. Walter was a man of few words and usually spoke only when spoken to, or if there was something *really* important that needed saying. Linda and I were on the shy side ourselves. It was a quiet lunch, the silence broken only by a light breeze that prodded the pines into gentle conversation. The pungent scent of the oranges we were trying to eat quietly seemed intensified and intrusive as it lingered in the still air.

Afternoon found us crossing a series of beaver dams. The horses were experienced at this tricky business, and so far so good—but then we came to an especially long dam at the outlet of a small lake. Walter decided we'd try swimming the horses across just above the dam. My dad had warned Walter not to try swimming the horses here, but the dam looked awfully long and treacherous, and the water looked deep enough for the horses to swim. It seemed like a good decision. Unfortunately the water wasn't as deep as it looked, and the bottom was composed of fine silty mud, commonly referred to in these parts as "loon shit." After a few desperate lunges, my horse Cindy was bogged down up to her withers. Standing on top of the saddle, I took a huge flying leap, chaps and all, and landed on the semi-solid footing of the beaver dam. Cindy struggled with everything she had in her and finally dislodged herself, but instead of coming toward shore, she swam out into the middle of the lake, no doubt wanting to put as much distance as she could from the boggy bottom. We watched helplessly from shore. Weak from her long battle in the mud, she wasn't swimming strongly and went completely under three times, saddle still on, before finally making it to shore. Her ears were full of water and hung straight down; if the situation wasn't so grim, her comical appearance would have been funny. Even after her swim in the lake, mud was caked under the saddle, and it and the blanket were sodden. I unsaddled her and cleaned her up as best as I could. She looked so pathetic, I felt bad about resaddling her, hanging my muddy chaps over the horn and climbing back on to continue on our way.

Not long after the beaver dam episode, the horses spooked, and there on the trail ahead of us was a mother black bear that had put her two cubs up a tree. Making a wide detour around the family of bears, we ran into heavy windfall and lost the trail. The horses were already tired out, and now they were having to buck their way through a wall of windfall. It was hard on us too, because we were each leading two horses whose jump wasn't always synchronized with the horse we were riding. I came close to being jerked right out of the saddle a few times. After one particularly spectacular jump, I noticed that my chaps were no longer hanging on the saddle horn. I had no idea how long they'd been gone. The thought in my head was, "Oh, no!—should I tell Walter or just forget it?" I screwed up my courage and told Walter. Without saying a word, he turned his horse and headed back the way we'd come. As if things weren't bad enough, poor Walter had to ride back through the windfall looking for my chaps. Linda and I waited in silence and the horses were happy just to stand and rest. Walter wasn't gone long, and amazingly, there were my chaps flung over the pommel of his saddle. He handed them to me without a word. I put them on and left them on.

The maze of windfall stretched on before us like a nightmare. It was starting to get dark and it was becoming obvious that we were off course. Walter checked his compass often and he looked worried. No one spoke. We were bone tired and so were the horses, but we had to push on—Dad was expecting us to arrive at the Big Bend that night.

Around midnight, in the light of a full moon, we suddenly broke into the openness of the Big Bend Creek valley. My feelings of relief and happiness no doubt paled in comparison to how Walter felt at that moment. As we made our way up the grassy valley bottom, my dad, who had heard the sound of approaching horses, appeared out of the moonlit night, striding toward us in his fringed buckskin jacket, his white cowboy hat gleaming in the moonlight—a sight for sore eyes. We'd made it to the Big Bend.

The pack trips of long ago were good times. Walter later sold his guiding operation to Doug Davis, and his ranch to George Bowers. Not long after, he married and moved to Atlin, where he established another guide–outfitting business. Burning out there, he decided to settle south of Williams Lake to ranch, before finally returning to the upper Nechako country, where his heart lay.

Walter passed away a few years ago, a mere shadow of his former self. But that's not the man I will remember. The Walter that is fixed in my mind is the ruddy-complexioned, barrel-chested guy who got us safely to the Big Bend that night so long ago.

SOME GUIDING STORIES

Uncle Stan guided for my dad for many years and has a few stories to tell. He remembers the time he was guiding a hunter named Eddie Fisher:

No, not the singer Eddie Fisher. We called him "little" Eddie Fisher because he had narrow shoulders and was kind of puny. But a nice guy. It was near the end of the hunt and Eddie still didn't have a moose. Eddie and I were walking the ridges on the upper Swanson, when I heard a grunt that sounded pretty close—I thought it must be a big bull moose so I said, "Get ready Eddie, here comes your chance to get a moose." Suddenly, up over the bank comes this big grizzly, not 20 yards away and coming right towards us, fast. I raised my rifle and all I could see through the scope was hair. My finger was on the trigger, just starting to squeeze down, when the grizzly turned and headed off down the hill. I turned to "Little Eddie," expecting to see him white faced and shaky, but he looked perfectly calm and hadn't so much as raised his rifle. In disbelief I asked, "Weren't you afraid that grizzly was going to get us?" Eddie said, "No, I knew my big-game guide was looking after me." Eddie had been casually enjoying the scene that was playing out in front of him as though it had been written into a script! My legs were shaking, so I sat down on a log and tried to roll a cigarette. Couldn't do it.

Stan believes the huge grizzly they saw that day was "Big George," the bear who'd been hanging out at the Big Bend for years. It's not that far across country from the upper Swanson creek country to the Big Bend. George was sighted many times after that in his favourite haunts, and was regarded with respect. Who knows, maybe he recognized Stan when he turned away that day, and held the same regard for him.

Getting meat out of the bush was often a tough proposition requiring some ingenuity. Hunting along the shore of a small unnamed lake, my dad and his two hunters spotted a moose and shot it just as it was about to enter the water, but the moose had made it to the deepest part of the lake before succumbing. Undaunted, my dad made a raft out of logs that he tied together with rope. He then poled the raft out to the semi-submerged moose and managed to get its head up on the raft. Drifting slowly toward shore, he unfurled the fishing line that he always kept in his pocket for occasions such as this—and caught four fish. When he got close to shore, he cast the line to the hunters and they proceeded to pull him in. The shore, however, was steep, so Dad ended up having to cut the moose in half in the water before they could get it out. The next day he carried a kayak to the lake and ferried the moose, bit by bit, down to its outlet end. There he broke the beaver dam to increase the flow of water in the creek and proceeded downstream in the moose-laden kayak to a spot where a branch of Lucas Creek comes in; from there it wasn't far to the road. After all this, he and the hunters still ended up backpacking the last of the meat out, but from then on the little lake with no name was called Kayak Lake.

Another grizzly encounter took place after Dad and a hunter had stayed the night at the Rum Cache cabin. They were walking out when they heard a loud grunting and, thinking it was a moose, stopped and waited for the animal to make its appearance. A moose didn't appear, but a grizzly did. Fortunately, the bear wasn't aggressive and continued on its way. Although at that time hunting grizzly bear was legal with the purchase of a tag, Dad never encouraged his hunters to buy one, because he didn't like shooting bear. Killing a bear in self-defence, or to protect meat, was one thing, but shooting a bear just for the thrill of it—no. On another occasion Dad and a client were walking along the trail near the Upper Cutoff cabin when Dad, who was in the lead, saw a bear bouncing along the trail, coming their way. He hollered, "Bear!" and then "Grizzly!" Turning, he saw that his hunter, who had been right behind him, was now hiding behind a clump of trees some distance away. Rather than being prepared to back him up if necessary, it was a case of every man for himself. Luckily, the grizzly turned and ran when he saw them.

There are grizzlies, and then there are pack rats. Pack rats are a fact of life in old log cabins in the bush. One time my dad was hunting with some clients and, since they were travelling light, he decided to stop at an old cabin where he knew he'd left some provisions. Upon arrival he shot a pack rat before turning his attention to mixing up a bannock. The hunters were hungry and saying how much they were going to enjoy the bannock. As Dad was mixing, one of the hunters spotted another pack rat running along an overhead beam. He shot it, and guess where it landed—right in the mixing bowl. After a few seconds of debate, the dead pack rat was unceremoniously lifted out of the bowl, and Dad continued his mixing. The bannock was cooked and enjoyed by all.

Mice are also an accepted fact of life in log cabins, especially those that aren't occupied on a regular basis. Such was the case with the Fish Lake cabin. Upon arriving back one night after a day of hunting, and as they were about to start supper, one of my dad's clients commented that there were mouse tracks in the morning's bacon grease in the frying pan. My dad assured him, "Don't worry, they'll go away when we heat the pan up." That must have eased his worries! Another time, a big bottle of homemade pancake syrup, kept in a gallon wine jug, was left on the table. Mice, attracted to the sweet smell of syrup, had managed to climb up the bottle and down into the syrup. But climbing back up was impossible, so the fate of the mice was sealed. The homemade syrup was thick and dark because of the Mapeline added, so no one gave it a second glance. Eventually someone clued in when they noticed some added ingredients, but by this time there were several victims in the bottle.

One fine fall day, Dad and Don decided to stop at the Fish Lake cabin to make a spot of tea. Don went down to the lake to fill the kettle while Dad lit the fire. When the kettle boiled, they couldn't help but notice how brown the water was as they poured it into the teapot. On closer inspection, they saw that the kettle was about half full of mouse droppings. They were really looking forward to a nice cup of hot tea, but decided not to have any that day.

Mice also like to get into flour, and occasionally pancakes were made before the tell-tale leavings were noticed. The hunters good-humouredly accepted these things as part of "roughing it," and it gave them something to talk about when they got home to civilization. No one ever got sick—and Food Safe classes were still in the distant future.

Mom remembers a certain group of hunters who liked to play practical jokes. One morning a hunter by the name of Dave Moore announced that he was going to make breakfast. He made corn pancakes. Most of the group thought they were okay, except for Ken, who did a lot of grumbling. When Dave went to feed the leftover pancakes to the dogs, there were none to be found. The next day Dave opened his suitcase and, lo and behold, there were all the missing pancakes, nestled among his clothes. Everyone had a good laugh, including Dave. Another trick of the breakfast cook was to embed the cardboard linings of jar lids in the pancakes. Everyone agreed that the cook needed some lessons on how to make his pancakes more fluffy—they literally tasted like cardboard! Another time, one of the hunters didn't want leftover pancakes fed to his dog, so he hung them on a spruce tree, like Christmas decorations.

There's nothing more refreshing than cold, clear spring water. But, mixing himself a pre-dinner drink on one occasion, one of the hunters added spring water from the tap to the whisky he had in his glass. As he was about to take a sip, he noticed a small frog in his drink. Dumping the drink out, he poured fresh whiskey into his glass and proceeded to once again fill it with tap water. There in his drink was another baby frog swimming around. This time he just scooped out the little animal and drank his drink, commenting that it had more flavour than usual. Dad and Mom have excellent spring water, but frogs occasionally find their way into the gravity-fed system.

A story with a different twist unfolded late one night when Dad was driving back to camp after having taken a client's moose to the locker in town. He was starting to feel pretty sleepy, so he decided to light up his pipe to help keep him awake. With one hand he tamped in some fresh tobacco and lit up as he drove. He was enjoying his smoke when suddenly a powerful explosion knocked his head back and all he could see was red. The truck veered sharply, but somehow he managed to avoid hitting the ditch. Coming to a halt, he turned on the cab light and tried to figure out what had happened. On his lap was the lead from a .22 shell. His pipe was split in half—apparently my brother Rick, who was about three at the time, had been playing with his tobacco and had laced it with some .22 shells. My dad continued on toward camp, now very wide awake!

Dad was seldom seen without his pipe clenched firmly between his teeth. Sometimes it was actually lit, though not usually—just recently an old friend told me that he once saw my dad with the pipe upside down in his mouth, intent on the job at hand. Uncle Stan told me this pipe story:

> It was at the old Hull cabin and Bert was tinkering with his outboard, tuning it up. Don and I were standing on the bank watching as Bert leaned further and further out over the water. Suddenly he leaned a little too far and tipped over into the river head first. When he came up, his pipe was still clenched between his teeth, a thin wisp of steam issuing from the bowl— just this little, crooked wisp of steam. Don and I cracked up— we thought it was pretty funny. Bert didn't find it too funny, though; as he came up out of the river he commented dryly, "I didn't think it was *that* funny."

I can understand why; it was his business and he had a lot of responsibility. Neither Don nor Stan were mechanically inclined, and so of little help when it came to keeping things like outboard motors running. Don and Stan were just enjoying seeing my dad slip up for a change instead of one of them.

Over the course of 50 years in the guiding business, only twice did hunters become lost. One of these times the wayward hunter was about 80 years old. He, another hunter and my dad were hunting out of the camp at the narrows on the reservoir and were at a small lake that was about a mile in from the camp. Since the octogenarian wasn't up to walking too far, my dad instructed him to cross the beaver dam and sit on a side-hill overlooking the lake until he got back. He further instructed him that if they didn't return in a few hours, he was to walk back to the tent camp for lunch and that he and the other hunter would meet up with him there. Here's how my dad tells it:

> The other hunter and I shot a small bull moose on the other side of the lake, and when the old guy heard the shots he decided to investigate. He walked in the direction he thought he'd heard the shots coming from, but missed us and kept right on going. After I gutted the moose, I walked back to where I'd told him to wait—to tell him we'd got a moose—but he wasn't there. I figured he'd headed back to camp but decided I'd better check up on him before packing the moose out. He wasn't in camp either. The other hunter and I walked back to the lake and I fired three signal shots, but there was no answer. We packed the moose to camp and he still didn't show up, so we headed back to the lake where we'd shot the moose. I searched the area for tracks and found some, but they petered out, so we lit a fire at the spot where I'd told the old guy to wait. The other hunter was a basket case, worrying about his old friend, and we spent the night on the hillside, listening. There was no sign of him by morning so I decided I'd better report him missing—at his age, he could have had a heart attack and could be lying anywhere. Back at the camp on the narrows, we loaded the boat and headed out. Once we were on the open water, I decided to cut the motor and fire one last signal shot. A response came from up the lake [the reservoir]. I took a compass bearing on the shot and headed back to shore. Using the compass bearing I started walking. I almost missed him because he'd left his camp and started walking again. When the old guy saw me, he called out, "Put the tea pail on!" He thought he'd walked back to the tent

camp. We were a long way from it. He'd been camped around the other side of a big hill, so he couldn't hear the shots I'd fired; the one he had heard was the one fired from the boat, which carried down the lake—it was quiet, real early in the morning, no wind. A week later I had to go back and put out a ground fire where he'd camped.

Oh, the joys of guiding!

The second lost hunter, Red, had hunted with my dad before. Knowing that he was good in the bush and a good walker, Dad gave him a bit of rope. They had stayed the night in the cabin on the creek that comes out of Hallett Lake and drains into Copley Lake. Here's how my dad relates the story:

In the morning we came down the creek by canoe to Copley. I told Red to walk about 100 yards in from the lake till he came to the outlet creek; I said we'd have some lunch there. I told him that if he hit Lorne Creek not to cross it because that would mean he'd missed the outlet creek. He never showed up. I waited all night with no grub, firing shots but didn't get any response. In the morning, I headed back to camp [home], ribboning the trail all the way—thinking Red might come across them. At Lorne Creek, I met Don coming up the trail. He told me that Red had pulled into camp the night before. He'd come across a fresh, running moose track and followed it so far he figured he might as well just keep going back to camp. They'd heard the shots I fired but didn't respond because they figured it might confuse me.

My dad was not a happy camper.

There were other occasions when things didn't go quite as planned. One of these involved Paul Angelo, from California—Charlie's son. Paul related this story to me:

My father had known Bert for 25 years before I met him—he'd hunted with Bert in the early '50s. Dad was to help cook for the hunt before us, and also help for my hunt as well. We stayed in the same home Bert still lives in to this day, on the Nechako River. First we hunted one day in the timber and one day in the swamp across the river. We saw one cow moose in the swamp and I noticed how fast it disappeared. Then Bert decided we'd take the "Scout" to Murray Lake, take a boat up Murray, then on up Cheslatta Lake and spend the night in an old cabin on the south side of the lake. It was cold and snowing, with snow on the ground. This was in October. The one element we didn't expect was a stiff wind that plastered our faces with snow as we moved up the lake. I remember a small island in the middle of the lake, which came in handy as the wind was blowing at 35 miles per hour. We beached the boat on the island for a little rest and baled the water out of the boat, then set out for the cabin, which we made before dark. Bert had no pipe tobacco, so he robbed a pack rat's nest for some willow and had his smoke before bed.

Next morning the wind had gone and it had stopped snowing; a good day to hunt. The plan was for Bert to drop me off across the lake so I could walk an old Cat trail that followed the lake a ways in. Bert would take the boat down the lake a few miles and meet me there. After getting instructions from Bert, I set off on my own—never having seen a moose before. I could hear Bert's outboard on the lake as I walked. The trail was narrow, with small clearings every several hundred yards. The rifle I was carrying was my dad's old pre-war model 70 .270 Winchester—I didn't know anything about ballistics, but Bert said it would do. The first clearing had nothing, second clearing nothing; then I looked up ahead, maybe 200 yards, and saw what looked like a giant set of moose horns. I raised the gun, got the moose in the cross hairs and fired, no hesitation.

Looking through the scope the second time, no moose; what the hell!? He had to be down. I ran toward the spot and there he was standing (or so I thought) about 50 yards away. I fired and down he went. When I got up to him, this animal was huge, much bigger than I had ever imagined. Another shot to finish. Bert had heard my shots and was on his way. I was feeling real lucky and congratulating myself when I spotted movement and another big bull running. At this point everything seemed to be in slow motion. The bull was running in the trees less than 75 yards away. With only a second to react, my mind did something funny: it said, "This moose is wounded: you'd better finish him off before he gets away crippled." So another shot. Well, two moose down. I headed back down the trail and met Bert already sharpening his knife as he was walking. We were both at the first moose and I said, "Look over there." He looked and said, "Aw, Christ!" I wasn't sure if he was upset because I'd shot two moose or because it meant there was so much work ahead. Bert put his tag on the second moose. There was no way to get the meat back to camp, not even in two days. We dressed the two and opened them up to cool and took off for home, first down Cheslatta and Murray lakes and then with the Scout over the worst road you can imagine—Bert's ability to keep that battered old Scout going is a story in itself. Back at camp Mary had a very welcome supper ready and it was a celebration with Old Style beer and me telling my story. The next day we would return to quarter the meat and start getting it and the horns out. Even with the four or five men, including my dad, we couldn't finish in one day. Young Stan Irvine went back the next day and finished. Now I know what Bert meant with his expression when he saw the second moose! I got to carry the horns out through the snow and trees back to the boat and into camp, just like in the magazines. Bert set me up and put me in position to make this successful hunt happen—I ended up in the perfect spot. Bert guided me into a great hunt, something I will never forget. My time with Bert and Mary was a once-in-a-lifetime gift from my father.

Several lakes in the area bear names my dad and his guides pinned on them. Some of them have become official, some not. My dad took Rich and his friend Gordon Guiberson to a little lake where he knew there were big fish; there was no road to it then, but the fish were of trophy size. After the Cutoff Butte fire, a road went by fairly close and locals started going in; they called the lake Hobson Lake, and so it is on maps today. Rum Cache speaks for itself; my dad buried a mickey of rum there and a year later went back, dug up the rum and drank it—putting Rum Cache Lake on the map. The Tea Pail was so called because my dad had a hunting camp there. There is a small lake not far from old River Ranch where the Hobsons (young Cathy included), ourselves and Don Hogarth used to go swimming on hot summer days. My dad started calling it Cathy's Lake, and the name stuck. Linda and her husband Lloyd live on Cathy's Lake now, and we still swim there. Then there's Hooter Lake, where a "real hooter" of a drink was concocted for a celebration at the end of a successful hunt. The drink consisted of wine, whisky and anything else that was available—mixed in with the campfire tea. The Kayak Lake story I related earlier. Bitch Lake? I forgot to ask about that one.

Life is seldom without tragedy, and just as guiding was getting into full swing in the fall of 1958, it struck our family. My dad's younger brother, Bill, was hunting near his old trapping cabin (my dad called it cave-in cabin) not far from Hash Lake when he was shot in the back by an American hunter. The bullet missed the blade of an axe he had tied to his pack by only an inch. Bill was killed instantly, leaving his wife Mary, two-year old daughter Maxine and newborn son Michael. The hunter had followed the newly slashed right-of-way that an oil company had cleared, going right by the door of Bill's cabin at the outlet end of Hash Lake. Wes was very bitter about the coming road and the changes he knew it would bring to his country; now, in a painful twist of fate, that unwelcome road had led to Bill's death.

Non-resident hunters didn't require a guide to hunt in Alberta, and this fellow, using a high-powered rifle, claimed he was shooting at whisky jacks. There was a trial, to which my dad and Stan went, but no charges were laid. Bill's death was, according to the courts, simply an accident.

After Denis Wood and I were married in the spring of 1966, we worked at banks in Campbell River and then Vancouver, where we requested transfers north. We transferred to Smithers in December 1968. By 1970, though, I was bored with my job at the Bank of Commerce in Smithers and, having no kids yet, I decided to hand in my resignation and go cook for my dad during the guiding season. It felt great to be back out in the bush again. Leaving the confines of the bank and the monotony of the work felt like getting out of prison. I wasn't the most experienced cook in the world, but I sure tried; I made every pie under the sun, and I remember at least one night when I had nine different varieties lined up for the hunters to choose from. My baked beans and baking-powder biscuits, however, left something to be desired. I don't know where I went wrong. The beans were as hard as bullets and the biscuits were like little rocks. The hunters were very politely and quietly trying to eat the stuff, but eventually they started making little jokes, such as the beans making good ammunition and the rock-like biscuits being so heavy they could be thrown clear across the river. I was young and embarrassed by my failure, but we all ended up having a good laugh over it. Maybe the pies made up for it.

During this same stint as cook, after making breakfast in the very early hours of the morning, usually between 4:00 and 5:00, I'd help get the horses ready. Being right on the river, it's often foggy in the fall and with the early starts that were required, there'd be just enough light to get around. Sometimes the horses were packed and saddled in the pitch dark using a flashlight. The weather was beautiful that fall, and I really enjoyed the time during the day when I was in camp on my own. One night all the clients were camping out, so it was just me and the dogs at the cabin. A pack rat had been coming in and making a nuisance of himself, jumping up and down on the tin dishes and making a terrible racket. I decided I'd had enough of the pesky critter so got out of bed and stealthily made my way to the kitchen with a flashlight and my loaded .22. I heard a noise coming from under the sink so quickly flung the cupboard door open and caught sight of the culprit. I fired two or three shots at close range and then shone the flashlight in to see if I'd killed him. But the rat I'd shot was already caught in a trap and had been dead for several days! Obviously the bad guy was still on the loose, and I'd just wasted some shells.

A JACK OF ALL TRADES

Trapping and guiding provided our family with seasonal income only, so in the summer my dad did carpentry and built log houses for several people in and around Vanderhoof. He worked on the construction of the new high school that began soon after our arrival in town, and he and Harvey Reeves renovated the Lejac Residential School. He made considerable renovations to Hobson's house at River Ranch, and helped Stuyve build his house. The construction of Culchoe-Nu and Nechako lodges, for which he was foreman, were projects that each spanned several years. There never seemed to be a shortage of work.

On one occasion Gordon Guiberson, Rich's old friend from California, was up for a visit, and he and Rich decided to go up to Stuart Lake (just over 30 miles north of Vanderhoof) to look at an island Rich had bought. They asked my dad to go along, but he was busy haying and wanted to get the hay baled and off the field. Rich and Gordon kindly offered to help so that he could go along for the trip. Jokingly, Dad said he'd pay them each a dollar a bale for their work and they took him up on the offer—though Gordon Guiberson was a multi-millionaire. When they finally got up to Stuart Lake to look at Rich's island, they stayed at cabins that Craig Smith had on a neighbouring island, in the middle of the lake about a mile from the shore on either side. Guiberson was so impressed with Stuart Lake and Craig Smith's island that he made Craig an offer on the place. Craig accepted, and Guiberson started planning his "Culchoe-Nu Lodge." Having to return to California, he hired a guy named McKane to find someone to build his lodge and look after the bills. McKane went into Bowman's Lumber Yard in Vanderhoof (where the Chamber of Commerce is situated today) and asked Bowman who he thought he should hire to build the lodge. Bowman said, "Get Bert Irvine to do it." My dad didn't have any other building contract on the go at the time so was happy to accept. He rounded up a crew of good carpenters, Jerry Swanson being one, and construction started in February 1966. Craig Smith Island (or simply Smith Island, as it is officially known now) is 20 miles up from the southern end of Stuart Lake, making the logistics of getting the construction materials in to the island, and the crew back and forth, quite a challenge. Ford Moran's 24-foot boat with a 50-hp Evinrude motor was used to get the men and some of the supplies to the island. My dad also hired the Hoys and Walter Dagenais to barge building materials up the lake, and he drove some of the supplies over himself in his truck, across the ice from the Native village of Tachie. An old Native gentleman from Tachie was hired to haul yet other building materials with his sleigh and team of horses. Stuart Lake is about 45 miles long and can get very rough in short order. There were many days when the crew was forced to lay over and wait for the waters to calm before striking out for Smith Island. The layover was usually in the bar of the hotel that looked out over the water—there must have been some bumpy rides afterward.

Gordon Guiberson must have had complete faith in McKane, because they apparently had little or no contact over the winter. When Gordon returned in the spring and went up to his island, he was surprised to find that it was Bert who was in charge of the project. The building of Culchoe-Nu Lodge, which took two years, involved the construction of 14 structures, including cabins and outbuildings, and a large dining room that was added on to Craig's original log lodge. One of the more interesting structures was a games building that practically hung over a cliff. It was a time that holds good memories for my dad.

In 1964 my dad took out an agricultural lease on 40 acres of natural meadow farther up the river from the Hull cabins. After beaver trapping the following spring, he moved "the blue bus," a dubious acquisition, up to the property; this would be home for my dad, my mom and the boys (Dewey and Rick) while they built the 30-by-30-foot log structure that would be both their new home and a lodge for hunting clients. By the end of the summer the spacious cabin was liveable, and preparations for the coming hunting season got underway. My dad made a log table, 12 feet long, that stretched across one side of the front of the cabin and afforded a view of the river, which runs within spitting distance of the front door. Rich's old barrel heater was installed in the centre of the cabin, and cooking facilities were much upgraded from the Hull cabin arrangement; there was the original wood cookstove we'd brought with us from Alberta, and a propane cookstove was also installed. One whole end of the cabin was taken up with a row of single beds to accommodate hunters or other visitors.

When I married Denis, whom I'd met while working at the Bank of Commerce in Vanderhoof (he worked at the Royal Bank), I was following in my father's footsteps in one respect; he had married a city girl and dragged her to the bush, and I had married a city boy and was doing the same thing. That summer, while on holiday from our bank jobs in Campbell River, we started a log cabin of our own. It was situated on the river at the mouth of Twin Creek, just upstream from Dad and Mom's. Denis got expert help in the art of log work from my dad. The following summer the two of them put up two more rounds of logs on the walls, then the roof support structure and finally the roof. Denis and I had a beautiful little cabin at which, over the coming years, we would spend a great deal of our holiday time creating cherished memories with our two sons, Neal and Russel.

The following year, 1967, after doing the necessary improvements under the agricultural lease, my dad was able to buy his property. But first it had to be surveyed, and this turned out to be quite a job. Bill Serle was the surveyor, but my dad and Denis did the chain work and line slashing. Denis and I had been given the go-ahead to buy our land as well—we had thought nothing of building first and buying the land later! Two birds were killed with one stone when the surveying was done for our 10-acre parcel at the same time as my dad and mom's. Denis recounts the task this way:

> [Bert] had found an old rock cairn on the other side of the river, marking the common corner of two district lots. He thought the cairn was probably built by Copley and Swannell when they surveyed the area back in 1909. Bill Serle had [Bert] mark the spot. He then took a reading with his transit indicating the distance and direction from the cairn to the place we decided our properties would meet. Then he turned the transit to the sun and burned two marks on a piece of paper, each exactly one minute apart. The positions of these two burn spots and readings taken on the cairn across the river somehow told him where on the map our two properties met. We then traversed the river and remaining perimeters, taking data every 100 yards or so. At the end of the day Bill would use an old hand-crank calculator to determine the location of our property lines, and when he was done, how many acres each contained. This information was then sent in to the provincial government so titles could be produced once the purchase documents were complete.

This antiquated method required much ingenuity, but worked well—a far cry from the high-tech methods in use today.
Denis continues:

> This work was done in June at the height of blackfly season. My job was chain-man. The long metal measuring tape to measure the length of each interval between points, called "hubs," has to

be pulled along. Part of the job was kicking aside the moss, and clouds of blackflies billowed out every time I did it. A stake had to be driven into the ground and a nail was driven into the top of the stake. I held the plumb-bob above the nail so Bill could sight on the string and take his readings before moving on to the next interval. [Bert's] job was slashing the sight lines so Bill could see where I was holding the plumb-bob. It was hot and the bugs were terrible! The job took about three days.

Twin Creek winds down a steep-sided ravine before emptying alongside our cabin into the river. My parents' acreage is bounded on the south side by a steep hill that runs the length of the property, so the ruggedness of the terrain, along with the hordes of blackflies and mosquitoes, made for a tough job.

In the summer of 1966 Fred and Betty Adams hired my dad to build a lodge on their property just east of the dam on the Nechako reservoir. Dad knew there were some good building logs on the road into Fish Lake, and, wanting to make sure all the logs were straight, he felled them all himself—enough 60-foot logs to build the 50-by-50-foot lodge that Fred and Betty had in mind. Using Fred's John Deere cat, they skidded the logs to a spot where there was a fork in the road—one branch went down to the campsite on the lake and the other to a trapping cabin of my dad's farther along the lake. Fred hired a logging truck, and my dad rigged up a gin pole to load the logs onto the truck. Everyone pitched in peeling the logs—Fred, Betty and their kids, teenager Laurie and younger son Normie. Frank Schumann and my brother Rick were hired to help peel and also clean and bleach the logs, using a mixture of linseed oil and diesel fuel. When the actual construction got underway, Fred lifted the logs with the loader on his John Deere cat as my dad swung them into position and did the notching. When they had the walls up to height, the Adamses decided they'd like to have two storeys, so another four rounds were put up. The roof had four gables, one in each direction, which with the four extra rounds of logs accommodated the upstairs. By that fall the lodge was usable; the roof was on, the windows and doors were in, and peeled poles had been placed over the chinking between each log. Dad also managed to get the plumbing done that first year, and over the next few years he built four cabins, all part of what became Nechako Lodge. Mickey Kelly was managing River Ranch for Jack Reid at the time, and he and my dad put the logs for the cabin floor joists through a mill at the ranch to square them off. Fred bought a load of milled logs, squared on three sides, for three of the cabins; only one of the cabins, the largest, is built from logs that haven't been squared, and these my dad and Mickey felled fairly close to the building site, along the shore of the reservoir. A few years after the lodge was built, my dad helped to put a full basement under it.

Sadly, Fred Adams suffered a fatal heart attack the year after Nechako Lodge was completed, and he and Betty didn't have the chance to live out their dream. After Fred's death, Buster Irving and Bert Snell went into partnership with Betty, leasing the lodge out to various people, Dick Collier being one. The lodge changed hands several times before finally selling in 1984 to Joe and Elisabeth Doerig, a young Swiss couple. They arrived with their newborn son Martin, and a few years later a second son, Thomas, was born. Both boys have successfully taken their entire schooling by "e-bus," the computerized version of correspondence courses. The e-bus program that now serves all of British Columbia was developed by the Vanderhoof School District. Joe and Elisabeth, now close friends of our family, have worked very hard and with the help of their boys have developed a thriving business. Forty years after construction, the lodge and cabins are still in good shape, and I think I'd be correct in saying that building the Nechako Lodge is one of my dad's proudest accomplishments.

Bert and his dog, Timmie, camped wicki-up style, at the mouth of Big Bend Creek, in preparation for bringing the horses out over the frozen Nechako reservoir.

Trailing the horses off the Big Bend meadows to the camp, in preparation for bringing them out across the ice.

Bert's herd of horses at "strawberry corner," one of their favourite hang-outs in the old days.

The tractor, loaded with hay, grain and gear, is ready to move out over the frozen Nechako reservoir to the Big Bend, on a horse-rescue mission.

Walter Erhorn's cabin overlooking Tatelkuz lake, packing gear hung on the wall.

This wonderful photo of Walter Erhorn was taken in the late '50s, during a month-long pack trip with Bert and the Rosen family into the Euchineko country.

Horses strung out on one of the pack trips with the Rosen family, from New York City. The foals alongside kept everyone entertained.

Freeloading moose help themselves to hay at Bert and Mary's place on the upper Nechako.

Bert (with hat and pipe) and Walter Erhorn on the Nechako reservoir, headed for the Big Bend. Walter keeps a sharp eye out for deadheads.

June Wood and Cathy Hobson on Prince, at River Ranch. Bert is at Prince's head.

Bert building another of his famous boats at the Hull cabin.

Bert proudly drives the homemade tractor that served him well for many years, bought from a farmer who lived south of Vanderhoof.

Bert and a good-sized bull moose in typical moose country.

Bert comes down Murray
Lake with a party of
hunters in boat.

Don Hogarth, Bert (standing, with one hand on the throttle) and Stan on the Nechako reservoir.

Don Hogarth throws a diamond hitch as he packs moose quarters onto Dixie, one of the Irvines' best pack horses.

Bert and Don enjoying their lunch outside rather than in the pack rat-plagued "fire-fly" cabin on the upper Cutoff.

Navigating the lower canyon on the upper Nechako.

A major undertaking—moving the outhouse at Bert and Mary's place.

Grandma Irvine loved "roughing it." Here, she and Grandpa Dave are at the Hull cabin with Rex, who managed to get into most pictures.

Don Hogarth, Stan and Bert (carrying moose head) load a moose into the infamous boat that was punctured by a snag in rough water on the Nechako reservoir.

River Ranch was home to author Rich Hobson, his wife Gloria and young daughter Cathy. This is the ranch house as it looked in 1958.

Chapter 7

RICH AND OTHER COLOURFUL CHARACTERS

Rich

In the summer of 1966, while at his beloved River Ranch, Rich Hobson had a massive heart attack that he did not survive. He was only 58 years old. Rich had packed a lot of living into those years, many of them tough ones in the Chilcotin and Batnuni country—years that no doubt took a toll on him physically. But after Rich bought Rimrock and then River Ranch, he turned his talents to writing and produced three bestselling books: *Grass Beyond the Mountains* (1951), *Nothing Too Good for a Cowboy* (1955) and *The Rancher Takes a Wife* (1961).

Drinking was woven into the very fabric of life in this part of the country in the 1950s and '60s—it was accepted bush hospitality that every pickup truck had a case of beer behind the seat, ready to be offered to whoever happened along. Rich was no exception to this way of life, and at any one time he was either "on the wagon" or he'd "fallen off the wagon." Once a party started it could go on all through the night and into the next day. There would be hot political discussions and debate on everything under the sun; contracts and deals were put together, and there was often a lot of singing—usually before Rich's wife, Gloria, and my mom, or any other women present, had thrown in the towel and gone to bed. Don Hogarth and my dad were always in on the revelry, and I remember well one night at River Ranch when Don played the same few tunes over and over again on his little concertina, punctuated with his inimitable giggle. We kids were upstairs in bed, and the music and the rest of the goings-on wafted up through the thin layer of ceiling boards, making sleep impossible.

Gloria loved entertaining, and there was always someone in town to entertain, such as Tommy and Marion Walker, on their way up to Spatsizi; Gordon Guiberson, Rich's old school buddy from California who had made good in his father's oil business; and Dr. Dietrich, another Californian. Even Pan Phillips showed up once in a while, and then there was a real party and reminiscing about the early days when he and Rich had first ridden into the Chilcotin country and started their ranch, the Frontier Cattle Company. Pan, along with some of Rich's other old friends from the Blackwater country, paid a special visit to Vanderhoof when Cathy was born in October 1952. Gloria's family from Vancouver came up to visit too; her brothers Jack and Fraser liked the frontier lifestyle and the change of pace from their lives in Vancouver. Fraser thought he might like to start a cattle ranch himself. Then there were all the interesting pioneers of the little frontier town of Vanderhoof and surrounding area— George Ogston, Sam Cocker, Pat Patterson, Maynard Kerr, the Smedleys and Elijah (Lige) Hargreaves, to name a few. Everyone was welcomed with the warmest of hospitality into the gracious Frontier House.

Rich was a real animal lover and identified strongly with his non-human friends. He attributed human-like personalities to his horses, dogs and cats. I've mentioned old Boswell, who stayed at Rimrock. At the same time Rich had three other big dogs, Habeas, Corpus and McTavish. Habeas was a German Shepherd–St. Bernard cross, while the bushy coats of Corpus and McTavish were attributed to the fact that they were part wolf. These dogs went everywhere with Rich and slept in his bedroom, even in the heat of summer. One of McTavish's offspring succumbed to distemper when he was about a year old, and Rich was devastated by his death. He buried him in a pair of red satin pyjamas he'd never worn—a Christmas gift. Nothing was too good for one of his buddies.

Rich was a true conservationist, and he considered his ranches wildlife preserves. He revered all life and was even known to brush ants off the chopping block before splitting wood. In the development of River Ranch, he had some land cleared on the river flats, but he clearly marked all the poplars that he wanted left. The groves of big poplars left standing were winter habitat for moose, and it wasn't uncommon to count up to 40 moose on these fields.

Rich was an ardent fisherman when, before the Kenney Dam was built, the river was alive with fighting rainbow trout. He kept a rowboat down at the river and would row over to his cabin (dubbed "Rich's Retreat"), which was high on a sandy cutbank above the river and its nurturing valley. Here he worked on his books and contemplated life. With luck he'd catch a few fish for supper on his way back across the river in the evening. Rich, like many people, was bitter about the diversion of the Nechako River and the effect it had had on the resident fish population. I don't think many people, including him, realized beforehand that the river would be reduced to a trickle during the years that the reservoir was filling, or that the clear water would turn to mud while the outflow carved its new channel through the Cheslatta River and Murray Creek. The provincial government had granted Alcan the conditional right to use all the water in the Nechako River in exchange for a promise to build an aluminum smelter at Kitimat, which would create employment. Neither Alcan nor the government talked about the downside of this massive project.

Rich believed strongly in the benefits of burning off the land in early spring. He and my dad would set out with a box of matches and before long we'd see smoke billowing up. One spring when Rich was burning off the wild meadows across the river by himself, the fire got away from him and spread into the timber. Rich reported the fire and a crew came out and quickly contained it while it was still relatively small, but the Forest Service sent him a bill for this effort nevertheless.

Rich hired the Erhorn boys and some local Natives to build snake fences and Russell rail (or moose) fences around the perimeter of most of River Ranch. Remnants of these fences can still be seen today, snaking their way through the trees and along fields. They're now rotting and full of ants, providing ready meals for bears out and about in early spring before the ground has thawed and other food is available. Rich would have liked that.

BREAKING IN THE NEW VET

The 1960s were a riotous, heady time. The guiding operation was at its peak, building projects were on the go, and it was always party time—I don't know how my mother put up with all the shenanigans that went on. One of these parties involved the local vet, Walter Wigmore, who was new to the area. In early 2006, Walter wrote:

About 37 years ago, after almost one year in Vanderhoof, and spring just beginning, I went to the Legion on a Friday night to drink and socialize. Fortunately I ended up at Bert Irvine's table, and he was kind enough to invite everyone to stay Saturday night at his place for a sociable sleep-over. Although this was odd by my former Ontario standards, where everyone avoids each other because of overcrowding, it is how a small community exists in a rustic bush environment, where everyone needs friends and neighbours to survive.

The next day, Saturday, a late group of us followed the rest of the party out to Bert's lodge on the Nechako River off the Kenney Dam Road. My friend Mike Lister, a teacher from England who was visiting for a year or two like the Irish "lay apostle" catholic nurses, and our young bachelor dentist friend and myself arrived two miles down the driveway to find it blocked by vehicles. We carried our gear and as much booze as we could carry down a long hill, around a huge bog-hole where the road wasn't anymore, and another mile down the road to the cabin. Too early for mosquitoes but late enough in the spring that the ice had been flushed off the river a few days before, we thirsty visitors sat outside and had some sociable beers. Towards evening, our booze was running low, so myself and Don Hogarth, a well-renowned horse trainer, wrangler and local character (one bare foot with a bow on his toe, walking home from the bar, etc.) whom I was most pleased to know, went off to get more booze from the vehicles. Walking that far seemed daunting in our inebriated condition, so Don suggested that we ride one of the horses. Knowing his excellent ability with horses, I readily agreed. My fuzzy mind thought how polite he was to suggest that I stand on a stump and hop on as he rode by. I was not even suspicious when he emphatically insisted that I not touch the horse's flanks with my heels. As he rode up to me, bareback in the dusk, I admired how high the horse held his head and pranced, high-stepping like a show horse on parade. As he rode by, the horse shied a bit as I hopped aboard behind Don and my left heel grazed the horse's flank. The jolt of electrical awareness that surged through me from the horse sobered me instantly. I could literally feel Don's total control of that horse on the verge of a wild bucking rodeo. As we pranced along with hardly a sideways skitter nor head drop, Don explained to me that this horse bucked and threw anyone that got on him, so he was training it to behave. However, this was only his second lesson, and he had never had two people on him before, nor for very long—and none bareback. That ride, with every second super-charged, was over in no time. I was instructed to dismount, without touching the horse's flanks, onto a stump, because if I just slid off the back or sides I would probably be kicked as he bucked. Unfortunately, the horse skittered one step sideways, my foot missed the stump, and Don and I both landed together in the huge, deep, boggy puddle at the bottom of the hill. Don, the consummate horseman, had kept hold of the reins. While he discussed things with the horse, in kinder language than I would have used, I went up the hill to collect the last of the booze. By the time I returned, Don was back on the horse, repeatedly making it go by the stump. With great trepidation, knowing I was the weak link in this arrangement—the second person to get on, it being almost impossible to jump on without touching his flanks, and with two cases of beer and a 26 of rye—I jumped on as Don rode by. Again, the electric jolt of perfectly controlled power, but this time with a wild exhilaration! Don had convinced the gelding that this was a wild adventure to be enjoyed, and that horse pranced so proud, just ready to gallop like a runaway. The ride ended quickly again, and although I lucked out getting *on* with the booze, I sure didn't when I got off. However, all survived except for two bottles of beer and my dignity. Don stayed on the horse, as this time I didn't knock him off by going over the horse's head—I took the usual route off the side, but upside down and on the off-side. I never could ride properly, but that rodeo taught me how to fall—I still limp occasionally. Don parked the horse, we all had a drink to celebrate the evening, then bunked down in our sleeping bags on "foamies."

The next morning before breakfast, as we were drinking the "the hair of the dog that bit us" (strange expression for a hangover cure, i.e., a beer before breakfast), I was asked if I had ever tried Tabasco sauce. Amazingly, I didn't know what it was, so I tried the spoonful they presented me with. It burnt something awful so I ran outside and stuck my head in the river. I drank lots of that cold river and kept dunking my fevered brow till I couldn't feel my ears and my nose turned white. After about half an hour with my head in the river, I was wet and cold with a burn in my belly, but able to stagger back inside. They told me to drink more beer to dilute it, but the more beer I drank, the hotter my belly got. It didn't take me long to realize that my beer now contained Tabasco sauce too! Breakfast solved the problem, though my stomach has been sensitive to hot spices ever since. I hope naivety isn't stupidity—just lack of experience, and experience is gained mostly by making mistakes, at least it seems so to me.

Halfway through breakfast, there was a loud, hair-raising scream from not too far away, and general opinion attributed it to a cougar till Bert looked out the window. A trapper was returning from his trapline now that the ice was off the river. He had taken his girlfriend with him for company during the winter. Obviously she had underestimated the hardship of a trapper's life—repeatedly harvesting furs from the trapline in deep snow on snowshoes, extreme cold, tiny log shack to live in, with a tin stove, cut your own wood, eat what you carry in (rice and beans) plus what you trap (ever try eating beaver or coyote or lynx?). And no laundry or washing facilities. It was the worst case of cabin fever I had ever seen. She sat poker-stiff in the boat as they rowed over through occasional small chunks of ice. She only did what he told her to, instantly, like a dog too well trained. Shortly after reaching shore, with all of us there to help unload the boat, she screamed again, then again and again as her focus shifted from him to us. Eventually Bert's wife Mary and her friends took her indoors and sat her down to adjust. The screams were greatly toned down to shrieks with occasional words, then to talking jags and shocked silence. They joined us for an excellent breakfast and she even helped with the dishes. After breakfast, we piled into a pickup truck that took us to the bog. We walked up the hill to the cars and drove home, thankful to Bert for the excellent weekend and life experience.

It was good to be us!

CHARLIE, BEN AND SYLVIA

After retiring in the 1970s, Charlie Angelo, my dad's first hunting client from back in 1955, turned his screen-door and window business in California over to his son Paul and bought a five-acre piece of property from Gloria Hobson. The property is located on a high river bench with commanding views up the river and across to the ridges to Bungalow Mountain on the north side of the river. It was here that my dad built Charlie's log cabin—his dream come true. Charlie would drive up in May from Menlo Park, California, sometimes accompanied by one of his sons or a nephew, and stay until sometime in October. For the next 20 years or so, every time he came he'd bring all sorts of stuff that he thought we could use: windows, doors, screens, bulk food and huge rolls of aluminum foil and plastic wrap, of which we all now have a lifetime supply. Later he started bringing bags and boxes of new and used clothing. We were never able to quite nail Charlie down as to where he got this stuff, a lot of which was of good quality. Some of it was outdated or far out, but trying it on was good for a few laughs. My mom would pull the boxes out when Linda and I came for a visit and then we'd start trying things on and give the men a fashion show. Each of us would pick a few articles we thought we might actually wear, but after a few years of this our drawers and closets started getting pretty full of what we termed "Fashions by Charlie." Mom ended up giving much of it to thrift shops. We think Charlie told the folks back in California that there were these poor folks up in Canada who just loved getting this stuff. If the truth be known, I'm still wearing the odd Charlie hand-me-down.

The first cabin my dad built for Charlie burned to the ground when it was only a few years old. A fellow who owned a neighbouring cabin, Ken Smith—known as "Smitty"—was burning bush piles down by the river and started a grass fire that swept up the riverbank and over to Charlie's. The cabin caught fire, and a lot of the big pines around the cabin went too. Dad built a second cabin (not quite as nice as the first one, I didn't think) that Charlie enjoyed for many years. That cabin is still in good shape, but Charlie is gone. He made it up for his last visit in the summer of 1999, but died later that year at the age of 86. His son Paul inherited the cabin and has been up a few times, but it's not like having old Charlie around. So many times, Denis, our boys and I canoed down from our place to his, and he'd be waiting with a treat—some food or drink—and would ferry us and our canoe back up to our cabin. We miss Charlie—not for all the goodies he brought up, but because he was part of our family.

Ben Stoyva came into the country from the Cariboo in the 1970s to work for Jack Reid at River Ranch. Ben was old by the time we got to know him, a Norwegian with a long white beard and hair to match. Rarely was he seen without his flat wool tweed cap on his head. His favourite drink was "wadca" and his favourite food was fish; Ben could frequently be found plying the waters of the Nechako for rainbow trout. After working at the ranch for a few years, he moved downriver a ways and lived in a neat little log cabin at Frank Schumann's place. Later he moved to a little travel trailer under a grove of big pine and poplar at the edge of my dad and mom's field, and there he lived for quite a few years, fishing and just enjoying the simple pleasures of life.

Ben played the violin. One day my son Neal and I rode up the field on horseback and pulled up at Ben's, just to say hello. Out he came with his violin and, coming up really close, looked into my mare Goldy's eyes and very earnestly serenaded us. No one was around with a camera, but what a picture we must have made. Once a day, my dad walked up to have a beer with Ben. Sometimes Ben would walk down—very slowly. He was hard of hearing, so most conversations were a yelling match. After you'd tried to get your point across, Ben would look you in the eye and, with his Norwegian accent, reply "Yaa"—whether he'd got it or not. Ben's daughter Sylvia Kelley and her family came out from Vanderhoof to visit him every other weekend or so, until she bought property on Greer Creek and moved a cabin onto it. She persuaded Ben to move down to her place and into a little logging-camp-type shack, right on the riverbank. On the outside wall beside the door Ben drove in some spikes, and there he hung several mugs with names on them: on one was written "Ben," on another "Bert," another "Charlie" and on a fourth one "Frank." Ben did drink "cofi," but somehow I don't think coffee was the beverage filling the mugs when his guests dropped in. Ben has been gone for quite a few years now, but the mugs are still hanging in their place just outside the door of his old cabin, ready to serve up some bush hospitality. Ben, Charlie, Frank Schumann, Don Hogarth, Ken Smith (Smitty) and Uncle Stan were all part of a group of older bachelors who were around the country in the 1970s and 1980s. They hung out together, and there never seemed to be a shortage of refreshments. There was always time for a party.

Over the course of the next 20 or so years, Sylvia herself became one of the colourful characters of the upper Nechako country, living alone in her cabin-turned-house right on the banks of the Nechako, where she watched the wildlife dramas that unfold along the river. My dad did some carpentry work for her, as did her son Brad, but much of the work on the house was done by Sylvia herself. She had a knack for decorating, and turned the little house into a masterpiece. Even in this modern age, Sylvia lived simply with none of the modern amenities. She had no plumbing, so all her water was carried by bucket up the bank from the river. She enjoyed her morning walk to her scrupulously clean log outhouse, which in later years was even outfitted with a wash stand and basin. Not having power, candles and coal-oil lamps provided her light. She was a voracious reader and loved to knit. Sylvia was a precious member of the larger upper Nechako "family," attending almost all birthday parties and other celebrations. Her passing on February 11, 2006, has left a huge hole in our lives.

CHAPTER 8

CHANGING TIMES

THE RIVER RANCH SAGA

I can remember Rich adamantly proclaiming, "River Ranch will never be sold while I'm alive!" He stuck to his word, but it didn't make sense for Gloria and Cathy to keep the ranch after Rich's untimely death. So Gloria sold the beautiful place, except for a few hundred acres, to Alfred Blundell, an Englishman who was head of British Mortgages. Alfred cut quite a figure about town in his fine tweed suits and a monocle on one eye. At about this time Jack Reid, a Californian, bought Stuyve Hammersley's place and within a year had bought River Ranch from Blundell as well. Now, including the land Rich had pre-empted on both sides of the river, River Ranch-deeded property totalled about 4,000 acres. Jack's plan was to run a dude ranch, and he did this with limited success for a few years. He brought his mother up from California to do the cooking and hired a few horse wranglers, including Don Hogarth, to take guests on trail rides. Sometimes my dad went along to tell campfire stories. Jack was apparently having financial trouble in the States, and eventually the U.S. law caught up with him. He ended up spending time in prison—for tax evasion, it was rumoured. Whenever Jack needed money he went to his friend Carl Koch, who lived in Prince George at the time. Carl and two partners owned a chain of tobacco stores and also some coffee shops. Apparently, Carl secured each of these loans with mortgages against various titles of River Ranch land—the ranch is made up of 31 separate titles. As time wore on, Carl ended up holding the deed to quite a few titles. Finally he bought the titles that Jack still held and River Ranch was his. Jack Reid had taken a lot of timber off the ranch to keep the place afloat financially. Carl, though, wasn't into logging. He hired a ranch foreman, Rodie Stewart, and for several years successfully ran a small herd of cattle. Eventually Carl ran into personal problems himself, and he and his partners were forced to sell River Ranch. This sale and resale of the ranch was to repeat itself in the years ahead, each successive buyer having his own dreams for the beautiful property.

In 1995 Carl and his two partners sold River Ranch to Mark Cramer, one of the principals behind Comprehensive Financial Services in Prince George, and to Wayne Brunette, a logger also from Prince George. Rumour has it that the purchase price was $2.2 million, and that Canfor (Canadian Forest Products) put up $1.5 million of that in return for logs. Soon after purchasing the ranch, the new owners did extensive logging, with no consideration for aesthetic or other values, in order to repay Canfor. They plowed through the scenic old drift fences and cut down every tree between the road and the ranch buildings. This did nothing to enhance the appearance of the place for their proposed eco-tourism business.

Mark Cramer set up venture capital companies and created a glossy brochure stating that "the setting is pristine." The plan was to operate a cattle ranch in conjunction with an eco-tourism business, a spa and a golf course. The brochure stated that they would log and clear up to 320 acres per year under the Agricultural Lease Program, thus adding to the existing 4,000 deeded acres. According to the brochure, the ranch had over 50,000 acres of grazing leases and "The Ministry of Lands and Forests is keen on moving this program forward on behalf of the Ranch."

Wayne Brunette left the partnership after most of the logging on the deeded land was finished. The original plan, to quote the brochure, was to build a "spa/resort with ten to fifteen luxurious suites, self contained with food services, spa amenities, a lounge and meeting facilities." This in itself sounds pretty grandiose, since the location is about 45 miles from Vanderhoof on a gravel road, with no amenities such as power or phone lines. However, the plan soon changed, and Cramer launched into the construction of a 45-room "lodge," which the promotional video implied had the backing of a major hotel chain. He seemed confident that because he was building his resort, the road would be paved within a year or so and B.C. Hydro would soon string power lines all the way to the ranch.

There were plans for a golf course to be built near the lodge, and in order that patrons not be bothered by "biting insects," the creeks and fields would be treated with a larvicide called Vectobac. Mark Cramer was dreaming big. His attitude seemed to be that owning River Ranch meant he could do to the country and its watercourses whatever he pleased. The Department of Fisheries and Oceans had other ideas and put the kibosh on treating the creeks. My husband Denis had appealed against the permits to spray the fields, since our property is adjacent. River Ranch money appeared to be in short supply by this time, and with the estimated cost of the treatments in the area of $30,000 per year, the permit was dropped. Then there was the plan to build a bridge across the river to access hayfields on the other side. Again it was taken for granted that they could just go ahead and do this—as if owning the property meant they owned all rights to the river itself. In the end this project too was put on hold, no doubt due to mounting costs.

Although part of the dream was not being realized, things *were* happening at the ranch. Under the able guidance of carpenter Len Heroux, Stuyve's old barn was renovated and turned into a first-class bunkhouse with a large meeting room/dance floor, complete with a kitchen in the hayloft. Stuyve's original house was still used as the main ranch house, and a house that Carl had built was for visitors. Another house was constructed to accommodate shareholders and other guests who were frequently there on weekends. A large stable with accommodation upstairs was built down the road at the old Rooker White place. An elaborate, labour-intensive network of two-sided board fences was built around the stable. A power line, strung between full-sized poles, carried electricity round the clock from a big diesel generator in the machine shed to the stable, a mile or so down the road. For a while, the place was humming. A lodge—now of 40 rooms, complete with basement and an excavation for a pool—was framed. A plywood roof was put on, strapped and all ready for the dark green metal roofing, the River Ranch trademark colour. But by 2000 the money had finally run out. Mark Cramer's sister and her husband were caretakers at the ranch for a year or so, and they would stop by once in a while. We'd hear that "the roof is going on in October." Then, "the roof is going on in April." We saw half a dozen dates come and go, but it never happened. Mark Cramer's big dream slowly collapsed, and now the aging skeleton of the lodge looms over the river like a huge prehistoric beast.

A cattleman from Armstrong leased the ranch in spring 2002 and ran about 500 head of cattle. Matt and Barb Mazzerieu, experienced ranchers from Vanderhoof (Barb is one of Eric Weinhardt's daughters) took charge of the cow/calf operation, but Mark Cramer cancelled the lease after one year. The cattle were hauled out, Cramer sold his herd of about 16 horses, and all the haying equipment and other farm machinery was sold as well. The ranch sat vacant until summer 2003, when Doug Brophy brought in some cattle to graze.

Over $13 million in investments in River Ranch Resorts (VCC) Corporation and other associated companies were sold before the B.C. Securities Commission started to investigate, tipped off by investors. The commission website names 13 companies that were involved in the venture, 8 of which are identified as being issuers of shares. At an early hearing, seven employees of Comprehensive Financial Services, who had been selling shares for Mark Cramer as part of their job, were fined. A hearing date for Mark Cramer, his son Michael and James Fortin was postponed several times. The hearing finally took place in June 2003 with the result that both were slapped with heavy fines and "barred from trading securities for twelve years for their personal accounts." The sale of River Ranch went before the courts and went through delays similar to those experienced in relation to the Securities Commission.

In spring 2004 the Marks, a family of lawyers from California, bought River Ranch, and although they were absentee landlords, they came up for visits several times a year. Their plans for the ranch were much simpler than Mark Cramer's. They improved the fields and cleared more land, planning to have a working ranch to which they could occasionally retreat. The reality was that River Ranch was never off the market, and with ill health in the family, the ranch was sold again—this time to a Korean-based company, the Dahn Centre. River Ranch has been renamed the "HSP Ranch Inc."—HSP standing for "Health, Smiles and Peace." In late 2006, it was a retreat for members of the many branches of the company that are scattered across the world. For how long is an open question.

THE END OF AN ERA

It is the proliferation of roads that has brought about the biggest change to the country. It wasn't until West Fraser Timber built the Holy Cross Road (completed in 1979), and Plateau Mills the Kluskus Road, that the landscape began to be altered significantly. Holy Cross Road leaves Highway 16 at Lejac, near West Fraser's mill, comes very close to the end of Holy Cross Lake and then continues on to Cheslatta Falls, where West Fraser built a bridge. To me the bridge is an ugly scar across the beautiful face of the falls—an aberration against nature. From the falls, the road carries on to the Kenney Dam, but many arteries—wide gravel roads—branch off it to access timber, their insidious tentacles reaching east and west into formerly pristine remote country. The year before the road and bridge were built, my dad, Dewey, Linda, Denis and I forded the river with horses just upstream of our cabin and rode through to Holy Cross Lake, Dad cutting trail and blazing as we went. As we neared the lake, we encountered the old wagon road that was travelled by the

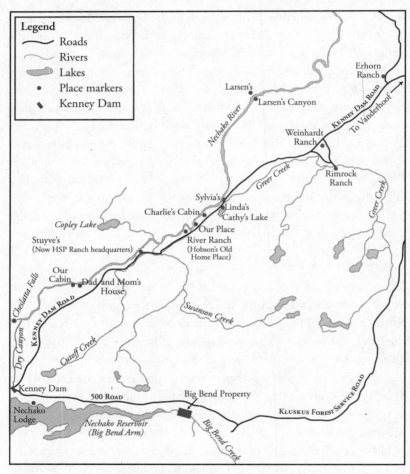

Upper Nechako Country in 2006

Cheslatta people before the dam was built—before they were flooded out and forced to leave their territory. My dad planned on using his new trail to Holy Cross in his guiding operation, but when West Fraser built its road and bridge the following year, the trail became useless; the country had been opened up and there was now a wide gravel road running close to the lake. Soon there would be large-scale logging. It was no longer a wilderness area.

Plateau's Kluskus Road lies farther to the south, and it too has numerous branch roads spreading like a spider's web across the country. Part of Kluskus Road, called the 500 Road, runs right by the Big Bend Creek property, and logging blocks line its perimeters. It's hard to imagine that getting there once entailed a boat trip, and harder still to imagine that the cross-country ordeal that Walter, Linda and I experienced used to be the only possible way to get horses to the Big Bend. The trails we took have for the most part been obliterated by logging, and a major road cuts through the heart of the country. A steady stream of logging trucks rumbles past the little road that leads down into the Big Bend, leaving it awash in dust.

A new major logging access road cuts a swath into the upper Cutoff Creek country—the area that we excitedly rode off into to explore our new trapline that sunny spring day in 1955. The landscape has been ravaged as never before—even more so than when great fires swept over it in past centuries—but in a different way, because of the building of roads and because the biomass (the trees) has been removed. Granted, the mountain pine-beetle epidemic has played a major role in the speed with which the landscape has been altered, but the rate of cut and whether or not it was sustainable was the subject of considerable debate even before the beetles hit.

Familiar words that meant home and our country to us—Holy Cross, Lucas, Cheslatta, Cutoff, Swanson and Big Bend—are now on the lips of every logging truck driver rumbling down the Kenney Dam, Kluskus and Holy Cross roads. It's strange to hear these names being said in such a dispassionate way by strangers on their truck radios.

In the 1950s and '60s it was not uncommon to count up to 40 moose on our way into town, many of them on the river flats around River Ranch. Now, if we see one or two we feel lucky. For years we've been told by the experts and by timber companies that clear-cuts are good for moose. True, the deciduous growth that springs up after logging—poplar, willow and red-osier dogwood, for example, and other vegetation such as fireweed—provides vegetation for moose to browse on. But then herbicides are sometimes still applied, and anything other than pine or spruce is still considered a "weed species" to be eliminated so as to prevent competition to the young pine and spruce seedlings. Herbicides aren't used as often as they used to be, mainly because of cost-cutting measures, but they're still used. And then there are the access roads, making moose more vulnerable to hunters and four-legged predators that use the roads as travel corridors. In the clear-cuts, moose are sitting ducks for the hunters, many of whom now use all-terrain vehicles (ATVs) so that few places are inaccessible to them. The answer to our dwindling moose population would seem to be in some form of access management or in cutting back on the hunting season until the moose have had a chance to rebound. The Fish and Wildlife Branch of the Ministry of Environment, however, maintains that wildlife populations are healthy, and government is not wont to decrease the revenue it receives from licensing and hunting fees. Wildlife biologists recently informed me, much to my surprise, that they aren't mandated to manage wildlife. Apparently their job is to regulate *society*—and they answer to the hunting segment of society, the majority of which wants no change to regulations despite a dwindling moose population.

Not only have dramatic changes come to the land; the formerly elegant old Hobson house has become a pack-rat castle, long abandoned by successive owners of River Ranch in favour of the newer houses farther up the river, at Stuyve's former location. Doors were left open and cattle wandered in, seeking relief from the flies. The kitchen now resembles a barn. The old McLary cookstove held its ground until a few years ago, when someone who wandered in decided it might serve their needs somewhere else. The little cottonwood that Rich planted and nurtured along, just outside the kitchen door, is mature now and spreads its branches protectively over the roof of the old house.

When the Cramers first bought the ranch, they planned to restore the house and operate it as a historic tea house. Like past owners, they did not see their dreams come to fruition, and I think the old place is past any hope of restoration now. It's sad to see it in this forlorn state, but once in a while we wander over anyway; I look at the house nostalgically, remembering its former elegance, Rich and Gloria and Cathy and all the characters that came and went through that welcoming kitchen door. I remember a time when the house reverberated with life and good times. Even the not-so-good times I remember with fondness.

It is the end of an era. My brother Dewey has sold the guiding territory that has been in our family for 50 years. My dad turned the business over to Dewey about 10 years ago, but both he and my mom continued to be a vital part of it right up to the end. Dewey just decided he'd had enough of it. The country has been opened up to such an extent that there are few places left to go where there isn't a road or a clear-cut. The wilderness as we knew it has vanished, and with it a way of life.

Allan Ray, the son of a Nechako Valley pioneer family, has bought the guiding territory. Allan already held the adjoining territory on the north side of the river, so it made sense for him to buy it. He in turn sold a portion of the area to Dan Brooks, who, with his family, owns and operates Crystal Lake Resort in the Greer Creek Valley. The guiding territory and its management is no longer in our hands. It feels strange, and a little unsettling, but in reality we lost any hold we might have had on the country years ago—to the timber companies.

The old homesteads, carved out of the wilderness by people who came to the upper Nechako area for various reasons—to homestead, to trap or to hide out from the law—have evaporated like mist under a warm sun and are now just a scant page in history. Most of the old cabins and barns have been burned or torn down; some are just slowly crumbling, roofs caved in and rotting into the ground. Soon there will be no trace of these hardy souls who once called the upper Nechako country home.

BERT'S TRUMPETERS

The temperature has to be at least −30° F for a stretch of several days before the Nechako River freezes over at my dad and mom's place. This is because the water coming over Cheslatta Falls, about six miles upstream, is relatively warm, having come through nearby Cheslatta and Murray lakes. When the weather turns milder, the river opens again. Overwintering trumpeter swans are attracted to the area because the open water allows them to forage for food, scarce as it is. Back in the early 1970s, my dad started throwing grain onto the shore ice to help the swans out a little—and the swans came through the winter very well, thank you.

Originally he bought the grain himself, but then the Vanderhoof Co-op started donating it, and continues doing so to this day. At first, when there were only a handful of swans, it was no big deal, since there was always a broken bag or two of grain at the Co-op feed store that they were happy to donate, but once several tons per year were required, it became a big commitment. The past few winters, when the Co-op grain ran out, Denis has hauled extra grain that several farm families, the Weinhardts being one, have donated to the cause. Being out of feed in cold weather with a big flock of bugling, hungry swans just outside your door can be pretty stressful.

Trumpeter swans were, not that long ago, on the brink of extinction. Edward Howe Forbush, a contributor to the book *Birds of America* (1917), says the reason for the rapid decline of trumpeter swans in the mid-19th century is obvious—they were an easy target and were hunted relentlessly for both their skins and their down. Here's how he explains it:

> The records of the traffic in Swans' down tell the story of decrease in the territory of the Hudson Bay Company. Just

previous to the middle of the nineteenth century about five hundred Swans' skins were traded annually at Isle a la Crosse and about three hundred were taken yearly at Fort Anderson. These were mainly skins of the Trumpeter Swan. The number sold annually by the Company slowly decreased from 1312 in 1854 to 122 in 1877. In 1853 Athabaska turned out 251, in 1889 only 33. In 1889 and 1890 Isle a la Crosse sent out but two skins for each outfit.

He was of the opinion that "the demands of fashion and the blood lust will follow the Trumpeter to the end." But fortunately for the swans, it was not the end. A ban on killing the swans was imposed, although Natives in the Arctic continued to kill them during the moulting season when both the adults and young are unable to fly.

The Edwards family, living at Lonesome Lake in the South Chilcotin region of B.C., began feeding trumpeter swans in the 1930s, and they are rightly credited with preventing the extinction of the great birds. Later, in the early 1970s, people like my dad on the upper Nechako and Leo LaRoque on the Nautley River at Fraser Lake helped the trumpeters get an even stronger foothold. Now a huge crowd of swans, varying from year to year depending on the success of their nesting season and the severity of the winter, shows up for dinner at my dad and mom's as soon as the river starts freezing over in its lower reaches. In the winter of 2004–5, the count was about 175—there are days when my dad wishes he'd never thrown that first handful! Tons of grain must be hauled out from Vanderhoof every winter to feed the hungry crew, even though it only supplements the swan's natural diet of aquatic plants. At Dad's age this is getting to be quite a chore. Two years ago, in early winter, he ran into Dave Geernaert, who works for YRB, the road maintenance contractor. Dave asked when he was going to start feeding the swans and my dad replied that he was thinking about not doing it anymore because lining up the grain, hauling it and unloading it was getting to be too much for him. Dave was really taken aback and immediately committed YRB to arranging for and hauling out all the grain, in a single load on a big flatbed truck. Now after all the years of worrying about being able to get the grain, and then having to haul it out, dodging logging trucks, over icy roads, it was delivered right to the door without even having to ask. It seemed almost too good to be true. There must be a moral to this story, but I'm not sure what it is. Maybe "You reap what you sow," or "It takes a village."

The swans have come to know and trust my dad, but they are nervous if there's a strange vehicle or person in the yard, and they leave if someone starts ripping around on a snowmobile. The swans also learned to trust my dad's old dog, King, though any strange dog sets off alarm bells. Sadly, King is no longer with us, but when still around, he could walk among them, "helping" to feed the swans. When only my dad and mom are there, which is most of the time, the swans will waddle up onto the porch and make themselves right at home. One morning my dad opened the chicken coop door and out rushed one very confused swan. Dad was given quite a start, not expecting the massive, flapping white wings and the swan's loud bugle of "Let me out of here!"

The swans are fed twice a day, every day, once they've arrived in late fall, and Dad, at 87, has started to worry about what will become of his swans when he's no longer around. He and Mom have suggested that Denis and I take over; not impossible, but it's a 25-mile round trip from here up to their place. An alternative would be to start feeding them on the river at our place, though the problem here is that the river usually stays frozen most of the winter, because we're farther downstream from the falls and the river is running more slowly where it passes our property. The other option is to just let nature take its course. We'll see, one year at a time. In the meantime, feeding time at my dad and mom's is a real spectacle to behold. It is not only the magnificent swans that come to dinner, but also an assortment of ducks—mallards, golden-eyes, teal and mergansers. Trumpeter swans have a wingspan of up to 7 feet 11 inches, and watching the beautiful birds circle and then come in for a landing is one of nature's amazing sights. We're held in awe, even after having seen the performance many, many times. Denis is still trying to get the perfect photo.

Feeding the swans is a big commitment, but it has been a very gratifying experience for my dad and mom. The majesty of the trumpeters adds great beauty to life on the river, and they hope their efforts over the past 30 years or so have helped these magnificent birds continue their steady climb back from near extinction.

THE FIRE

We had a forest fire in June 2004. That Father's Day was another sunny day in a long string of sunny days, and we had all gathered at my mom and dad's to celebrate. The first little bit of smoke seemed innocent enough, but by that night we were all on full alert. Just to be on the safe side, Mom went into town with Dewey's wife, Cindy. By the next day we had a full-scale forest fire on our hands. Since the fire started in the Nechako Canyon, it was close to dad and mom's, and our cabin on the creek. Our own place was like Grand Central Station—the yard was crammed with vehicles and every bed was taken. A total of five dogs, two of them pups, were also under our roof. From our living-room window, looking west that night, the fire appeared to be bearing down on top of us, but in reality it was still many miles away, ferociously sweeping through the beetle-killed pine forest just south of my parents' place.

No one under our roof got much sleep those first two nights, imagining that all was lost farther up the river. A fatalistic attitude was beginning to set in—things were out of our control, and if the cabins burned, we'd simply rebuild. Very early on Monday morning the men drove up for a look while I stayed behind to babysit the dogs. Later that day, the Kenney Dam Road was closed and my dad and Dewey came to our place by boat, down the river. The fire had jumped a guard and travelled north, across my parents' road to the ridge just above their place. We were a grim-looking crew sitting around the table that night.

The next morning we headed back upriver in the jet boat, not knowing what to expect. We came around the last corner, and there was my mom and dad's cabin, enshrouded in a strange yellow haze of smoke and mist as Forest Service sprinklers pelted river water on the house and yard. That scene, and the feeling that came over me, is forever etched in my memory.

Miraculously, the old log house was dry inside, and I set about making coffee for the weary-looking firefighting crew, straggled about the yard monitoring the sprinklers. Since the area was on evacuation, we didn't know if we'd be allowed to stay, but they didn't say we couldn't and we didn't ask. Denis took over keeping the water pumps fuelled and running, while my brothers, Dewey and Rick, ferried firefighters up the river in the jet boat. My dad sat in his big red rocking chair looking very weary—but of course not too tired to recount his firefighting days of old to the coffee drinkers.

The whump-whump of helicopter blades overhead and the constant communication between crews on the fire channel of the radiophone became commonplace—it was like a war zone. The fire had swung around behind the property and trees were exploding like rockets along the ridge behind the hayfields. Denis, Dewey and Dad stayed down at the place for most of the following week, but Rick had to get back to his job in Prince George after a few days. Denis spent most of his time hosing down the fire as it crept ever closer to our cabin—finally, when it was just across the creek, he and Dewey cut down all the big spruce trees between the creek and the cabin. It was a desperate measure, but in the face of fire you make a decision and then just do it.

With Denis away helping fight the fire, I was on "cow-watch" here at home. Denis had been working on our fences when the fire broke out and hadn't been able to finish the job. As a result, Brophy's cattle kept getting into our precious hayfield. Mom could only take two days of being in town before she wanted to be where the action was, so she was here with me. We made a scary trip to deliver groceries to my dad and Denis, travelling through thick smoke and still smouldering fire, and returned to a large herd of cows milling around the barn. I dashed off to get Linda and Lloyd, thinking we'd need help with this bunch, and as I drove back down the driveway, there were all the cows heading for the exit gate to the river. Someone was walking behind them with a big stick—it looked like Mom. It *was* Mom. She'd put the cows out single-handedly. What she didn't know was that the huge brute of a bull was walking right at her heels. He'd been standing in the barn, and she didn't see him come out; being hard of hearing, she didn't hear him fall into line behind her!

Eventually, after the wind changed several times and the fire was more or less out of control, we awoke to the pitter-patter of rain falling gently on the roof. That was the beginning of a week or more of good steady rain. The fire crew was left to put out the hot spots, and we were left to get our lives back in order. Initially, the rumour around town was that my mom and dad had been burned out on the first day of the Kenney Dam fire. The tongue-in-cheek rumour circulating around town, I was told, was that "the fire got so close it singed Bert's beard off!"

Two bushmen: Bert and Ben Stoyva outside Bert's cabin.

Buddies Ben and Frank
Schumann at Bert and
Mary's.

Considered one of the
family, Charlie Angelo helps
Lisa, Dewey and Cindy's
daughter, cut her birthday
cake.

Bert during a hunt in 1988, his trademark pouch of Sail tobacco tucked in the front of his overalls.

Bert and son Dewey, satisfied with a successful hunt.

A beautiful fall day in upper
Nechako country; Bert
paddles down Rum Cache
Lake with a client.

Swimming the horses across the Nechako River in high water to cut trail to Holy Cross Lake. The photo was taken was before the bridge was built across Cheslatta Falls.

Bert's chicken coop in all its glory.

For years, Bert has fed the trumpeter swans that arrive on the upper Nechako.

A trumpeter swan comes for a visit.

Christmas 2002, at June and Denis Wood's place. Bert is dancing with April (Linda's granddaughter), while Linda's daughter Nadine plays the accordion.

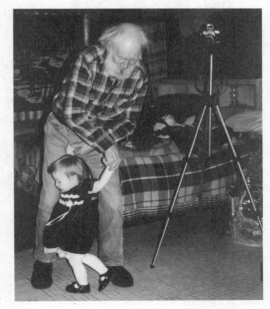

Bert dances up a storm with June and Denis Wood's granddaughter, Ava, at Christmas 2002.

Bert and Mary Irvine in their home on the Nechako, 1998.

STILL DANCING

Feeding the swans, making hay, feeding two horses, and cutting wood and getting it into the house all contribute to keeping life busy and interesting for my dad and mom. They still grow a big garden and have a greenhouse with a wood heater that my dad gets up and lights in the middle of the night if the sensor sends out the alarm that the temperature is getting close to freezing—something that happens frequently out here. For many years they kept a flock of chickens, mostly my dad's undertaking, and fresh eggs were delivered right to our door every Monday morning—until recently, when a mink got into the coop and killed every last bird.

You would think that living 50 miles from town, life would be quiet. In winter, yes, but in summers past this has not been the case. It's been said that the Nechako is the most studied river in the world, and since my dad and mom's place is the first below Cheslatta Falls, both the Department of Fisheries and Oceans (DFO) and Alcan established water temperature and flow gauges there. Alcan's consultants, first Envirocon and then Triton, made it their headquarters for research and monitoring of the chinook salmon. Starting in early spring, the river became a beehive of activity. One year my parents even allowed a viewing platform to be put up on the roof of their house. The DFO had a viewing platform in a big cottonwood beside Dewey's cabin, as well as platforms on trestle-like structures in the river itself. For many years my dad and mom recorded water and air temperature, and took photos of ice conditions on the river for DFO. At one time you couldn't go to their house without finding a DFO or Triton employee, usually a young person, sitting at the table having a cup of coffee and a cookie, and often playing a hand of cribbage with my mom. Some of these people became good friends over the years. In 2006, for the first time in about 30 years, Triton, Alcan's consultants, didn't set up camp in the yard. DFO employees still do some monitoring in the summer, but things are pretty quiet now, and in a way, Dad and Mom miss all the activity.

There are, however, always those unexpected events that keep life interesting, like the night a bear ventured into the cabin. Hearing strange noises, my mom woke up to see the bear strolling toward the kitchen. She yelled to my dad, "There's a bear in the house!" He came back with, "No, it's just one of the dogs." The night was warm, so they had left the inner door open, and the bear had ripped the screen off the door. Luckily, all the yelling spooked the bear, and he ran out the same way he'd come in. My dad grabbed his rifle from the gun case and headed out into the night. King, who had come out from his place under the bed by this time, waited from the safety of the porch, craning his neck around the corner as he peered into the dark. When my dad came back, he looked at him as if to say, "Didn't get him, eh?"

King was quite a dog. He was about three months old when Rick rescued him from an animal shelter and, thinking he'd make a good dog for my dad, brought him out. According to Rick's friend who ran the shelter, King was a husky–wolf cross. He looked like it, and he had the gait of a wolf—sort of a long lope that looked slow but covered a lot of ground. King grew into a fine-looking specimen, and liked to sit with one paw on my dad's knee while gazing into his eyes.

One winter day my dad looked up the frozen river to see King hightailing it for home with a pack of 9 or 10 wolves hot on his heels. He'd been playing with the wild canines when they turned on him, as so often happens. Dewey, who happened to be there at the time, jumped on a snowmobile, shot the lead wolf, pulled alongside King and, without slowing his pace, King hopped on behind him—and all without losing his dignified expression for a moment.

Every spring my dad goes to the convention of the B.C. Trappers' Association and dances up a storm, not satisfied until he's danced with every woman there. A few years ago he was given an award in the form of a mammoth crib board made from a slab of yew wood two inches thick. At one end of the board is a plaque that reads: "Bert Irvine, Longest Consistent BCTA Member, Presented at 100 Mile House, March 17, 2001." The crib board, handmade by Ken Pezzot, a trapper from Vancouver Island, is a real work of art. When presented with the board, Dad of course had to play a game of crib with Ken—which he won. At home he never plays, however; it's Mom who is the expert, and most people who come through the door challenge her to a game.

At Christmas and other special occasions, Linda's daughter Nadine plays the accordion and her husband, Gord, plays the guitar, and we all do a little dancing. A few Christmases ago my dad gave my little granddaughter Ava a whirl. At one and a half years old, she was game to dance with her still jiving 83-year-old great-grandpa.

The country has changed here in the upper Nechako, and it will change some more, but life is still beautiful. As if to confirm that this is so, a whisky jack has just floated down onto an outstretched branch of the spruce tree by my window, as I gaze toward Bungalow Mountain and the river. Yes, the river. Not the river it was or could be, but still flowing. The much-needed, healing rain finally arrived last night, and a light mist veils the top of Bungalow. This is good; we will be picking blueberries this year after all.

A dog's-eye view of Upper Nechako country; this is June and Denis Wood's dog, Dusty.

Born in Winnipeg, June Wood grew up largely in Vanderhoof, B.C., where her father, Bert Irvine, had a trapline. Here, in the pristine beauty of upper Nechako country, she formed a deep and lasting connection to nature and to the Nechako River. She has been involved in many conservation initiatives over the years, including a fight to save the Nechako River from further diversion. She and her husband, Denis, live on an acreage southwest of Vanderhoof and operate a small nature-based tourism business.